All God's Children Are Lost, But Only a Few Can Play the Piano

SHELDON KOPP

❧

*All God's Children
Are Lost,
But Only a Few
Can Play the Piano*

❧

FINDING A LIFE THAT
IS TRULY YOUR OWN

PRENTICE
HALL
PRESS

New York   London   Toronto   Sydney   Tokyo   Singapore

All accounts of patients are disguised to protect their privacy. In some instances, the portraits I have presented are composites and in others, identifying biographical details have been either omitted or changed.

Copyright © 1991 by Sheldon Kopp

PRENTICE HALL PRESS
15 Columbus Circle
New York, New York 10023

PRENTICE HALL PRESS and colophons are registered trademarks
of Simon & Schuster Inc.

Library of Congress Cataloging-in-Publication Data

Kopp, Sheldon B., 1929–
  All God's children are lost, but only a few can play the piano:
finding a life that is truly your own / by Sheldon Kopp.
      p.   cm.
  Includes bibliographical references.
  ISBN 0-13-026881-X
  1. Life. 2. Kopp, Sheldon B., 1929–   . I. Title.
BD431.K63   1991
128—dc20   90-53703
                                                          CIP

Designed by Victoria Hartman

Manufactured in the United States of America

First Edition

10   9   8   7   6   5   4   3   2

Contents

O you followers of Truth! Do not be deceived by others. Inwardly or outwardly, if you encounter any obstacles, kill them right away. If you meet the Buddha kill him. . . . Do not get yourself entangled with any object, but stand above, pass on, and be free!

—*Lin-Chi*

I am determined to let myself be transformed by the sounds arising out of the stillness of my soul and to allow my heart to call the tune to which I dance my life.

—*Sheldon Kopp*

Prologue
The Breaking of the Vessels

There was a time when a bewildered and beleaguered people asked, "If God is everything, how can there be a world?" and "If God is 'all in all,' how can there be things that are not God?"[1]

Finally, they decided that an obscure legend held the answers: In the beginning, God withdrew Himself into Himself[2] to make room for the universe. In the space provided by his withdrawal, He created the configurations that were to make up this world and filled each one with divine light. Some of these forms were too fragile to contain the awesome power of His holy fire and so they shattered. The breaking of the vessels created a cosmological crisis. Each scattered fragment contained a divine spark. To gather these sacred sparks together again was to become the people's task in the world.

The legend of the breaking of the vessels became popular at a time when the people were undergoing an awful testing of their faith. They had endured unremitting oppression for so long that they despaired of ever being saved.

In desperation, they turned to autocratic interpreters of their religious law who assured them that if only they would do as they were told, all would be well. Obedient submission to these dogmatic custodians of tradition left them helplessly dependent, unable to decide for themselves what was truly right for each particular one of them.

When patient obedience to their religious authorities didn't improve their desperate conditions, the people tried trusting the prophecies of self-proclaimed seers. The fortunetellers assured them that their worries were over, because the length of their suffering was a sure sign that the long-awaited arrival of the Messiah was at hand. Gullibly accepting these messages as magic, the people waited to be saved, still unable to figure out on their own how to live their lives.

Although they continued to suffer in the years that followed, their savior did not come. In the end, they realized that whether they depended on authority or on magic, they remained lost and alone.

Where were they to turn? Finally, a mystical group offered a practical but liberating and soul-fully relevant approach to life, inspiring spiritual growth in everyone it touched. This new approach taught that the people could trust themselves to

live their own lives because "everything is funda-
mentally open to all, . . . is so simple and concrete
that each man of real faith can grasp it."[3] In other
words, ordinary human beings would simply live
their everyday lives with heartfelt devotion and
God would be pleased. When the people understood that everything that mattered in life was
open to everyone, they no longer needed anyone
outside themselves to guide their actions or interpret their experiences.

The mystics expanded the legend of the breaking of the vessels to make a place for everyone by
pointing out that we each have a higher power
within us. By simply carrying out everyday activities and undertaking every act with soulful dedication, each person can affirm life for God's sake by
liberating the divine sparks that exist within each
of us everywhere.

We all have something precious to offer—something that exists in no one else. When we turn
lovingly toward whatever stirs our hearts, our personal treasures are revealed, and this becomes our
way of rejoicing in God.

This miracle is made clear in a tale told of several learned men who visited a teacher of this mystical way. The teacher asked them, "Where does
God dwell?" Laughing at him, they replied, "What
a thing to ask! Is not the whole world filled with
His glory?"

Because the teacher could see that the visitors did not understand, he answered his own question by saying, "God dwells wherever people let him in. But we can let Him in only where we really stand, in a place where we live a life that is truly our own."[4]

PART I

❧

Crises as Opportunities for Discovering Our True Selves

Do not conform any longer to the pattern of this world, but be transformed by the renewing of your mind.
——*Romans 12:2*

My work on myself cannot be completed in one lifetime.
——*Sheldon Kopp*

1

"I See," Said the Blind Man

Twenty years ago I encountered a crisis so unsettling that, at the time, I couldn't see how anything good could possibly come of it. Unexpectedly, I became so seriously ill that the doctors predicted my life would be much shorter than it has since turned out to be.[1]

After I had recuperated from my first operation, our oldest son returned home from college for the break between his first two semesters. Demonstrating that he was determined to make his way on his own, for several weeks Jon moved in and out of our lives. Near the end of his college break, he made sure to find me alone in my study one evening so that we could discuss privately how each of us felt about my not having long to live.

Our tearful, loving exchange was both emotionally painful and powerfully liberating. Jon seemed comforted when I said that I had begun to come to terms with dying and that I was devoting myself to enjoying what life I had left.

In turn, more clearly than ever, I realized how much I loved him as a son. I also came to see that, were I younger and not his father, I would have cherished him as a friend. And if he were older and not my son, I would have been happy to have had a father like the man he was on his way to becoming. All of these paradoxical permutations and combinations of thoughts and feelings made me more aware that now my mission was to become a more loving person—to myself and my family—in the time I thought I had left.

Soon after our talk, Jon left home to return to school. A few days later, he sent me a short note consisting only of a story that he had come across about a blind jazz musician whose piano playing we both enjoyed:

Relaxing between sets in a 52nd Street bar, Art Tatum sat alone at a table, drinking beer from a bottle. A missionary wandered in from the street and came over to talk to him.

She said, "Joining the flock is your only salvation." Without answering, Tatum took another swig of beer.

"If you don't join the flock, you'll be a lost child of God," she insisted. Art went on sipping his beer.

When the musician decided that the evangelist had pestered him long enough, he shrugged and answered softly:

"All God's children are lost, but only a few can play the piano."

4

I understood the message Jon had sent me. Not only did I feel more alive now that I was facing death but as the blind piano player could "see" his uniqueness, this crisis had allowed me to appreciate all that is singular about who I am.

Facing our own death is the ultimate experience of feeling lost and alone. But encounters with our mortality aren't the only occasions we have for searching our souls. Opportunities to live more in accord with who we truly are occur in each moment of our lives—although they do intrude more clearly on some occasions than in others. From time to time, we all experience predicaments for which we cannot prepare completely. Often, we are willing to settle for relief from stress. When we do, all we can hope for is getting back to business as usual as quickly as possible. Yet when we look for a quick fix, we miss out on whatever increased self-awareness we might have gained.

If, instead, we understand each crisis as a crossroads, we have the option of turning the disruption into a choice-point. The way we deal with the disarray in our lives can determine decisive changes—for better or for worse. *Instead of dwelling on the unfairness of whatever has happened to us, we can focus on our freedom: We can try to learn whatever our crisis has to teach us and to choose from among any options it might disclose.*

Here are a few examples of the sort of situations I have in mind. From time to time, we all go through identity crises—occasions when we question who we really are. Ironically, our uneasiness may allow us to explore how different we are from other people and so to recognize their singleness, as well as to see just how much we all have in common.

5

In our efforts to be reasonable, normal, sane, popular, or just one of the crowd, often we end up settling for relationships that are more social than personal, more ceremonial than spontaneous, and more superficial than intimate. When we ignore our idiosyncrasies and mask our own particular way of experiencing life, we shut others out. If we are willing to be open about our thoughts and feelings—no matter how irrational they may seem to us at the time—we stand nakedly revealed, instead of cloaked in costumes that misrepresent us for fear of exposure. *When we avoid revealing our true selves to others, we fake our image in ways that may fool ourselves as well.*

We all undergo recurring crises of faith when everything we believe in is called into question. If we are bold enough to follow our doubts to the edge of emptiness and uncertainty, we may discover that trust in what we believe has deepened. *Only by allowing and enduring this holy insecurity can we stay in touch with the higher power that is otherwise hidden within us.* Once we begin to risk living openly and in good faith, we may lose interest in trying to figure out what's right and what's wrong and get on with living a life that is worthwhile to us, regardless of what it might mean to others.

At some points along the way, particularly at midlife, most of us come upon existential crises that challenge what our lives are all about. If we dare to reexamine with relentless honesty just how we have been living, we can reshape our lives by consciously choosing to live according to our own values and desires. Then we will become too busy living in our own singularly meaningful way to waste time worrying about the ultimate meaning of life.

Although it is clear that our childhood contributes to

shaping our personalities, we are all subject to other influences that we will encounter well after we're grown. Children who have been well prepared emotionally develop a comfortable sense of who they are. When the time comes to accomplish the tasks of finding mates, building careers, and raising families of their own, they know how to take care of business.

But after we've reached success in attaining traditional, practical goals, and even if our lives seem to be going well, there will be times when each of us feels unsettled enough to ask ourselves, "What does it all mean?" and "Is this all there is to life?" The restlessness underlying these nagging questions indicates an underlying crisis of faith. If we are to resolve this uneasiness and make sense out of our uncertainties, we first must recognize our upset feelings for what they are—*the hungry outcry of an unsatisfied soul*. It is an inner voice to which we must attend again and again every day of our lives.

The situation is clearly seen in ordinary situations like the scene Joseph Campbell relates of a family seated at the dinner table. The father tells the son to drink his tomato juice, but the son refuses, complaining that he doesn't like tomato juice. When the father angrily repeats that the boy must do as he is told, the mother pleads, "Don't make him do what he doesn't want to." The father scowls at her with contempt and admonishes, "He can't go through life doing what he wants to do. What would happen if people just did as they pleased? I always try to do what I'm supposed to do. *I've never done a thing just because I wanted to in all my life.*"[2] What a pathetic statement for a middle-aged man to make!

The inner yearnings of midlife crises cannot be fulfilled by having another child or getting a promotion. Extramarital affairs and career changes may serve as temporary distractions, but they won't relieve our anxiety that our lives are incomplete.

These are the times when we must consciously listen to the voice of our inner selves. Instead of escaping into distracting activities that serve as temporary pacifiers or simply doing what is expected of us, we must begin paying attention to our personal longings and commit ourselves to pursuing experiences and activities that make our lives feel more meaningful. However, rarely can we accomplish the inner transformations needed to put us at peace with ourselves so that we can "follow our bliss"[3] without enduring temporary periods of turmoil, disruption, and isolation in the process. Yet, if we are willing to suffer some lonely soul searching, we can change what we do and how we feel.

Many people play it safe, accepting conventional guidelines for living. They avoid the risks of exploring their inner selves by following socially sanctioned paths, trying to fill their inner emptiness with prized material possessions and popularly acclaimed achievements. Often, their superficial sense of security is purchased at the price of missing out on the unique rewards of venturing alone into the darkness of their souls and exploring the unknown territory where they might discover unforeseen options for living in more colorful, creative, and ultimately more satisfying ways.

If we choose to undertake the search for answers to our unrest, we must give up our hold on what we find familiar while reaching out for what is as yet unknown. It is a time when even the most confident of us may feel the need for some support from others, but much of this journey must be made alone.

We often feel reluctant about delving too deeply into unknown aspects of ourselves, as if afraid we'll uncover dark horrible secrets or let loose demons that will get out of control. We hang back for fear that we might get so lost that we would never be able to find our way back home. Some of us are sufficiently vulnerable that while we are overcoming our needless fears we may need professional helpers and guides along the way. Even so, we need to be careful about whose help we accept, choosing as our primary guideline whether or not they are interested in our becoming our own sort of person.

Rather than pursue our own personal vision, we may ask authorities for instructions or follow paths that are popular among our peers. If, instead, we assume full responsibility for deciding how we will live our lives, we risk wrestling with our inner demons, but we will be freed of the complacency that makes us miss out on just how singular our selves can be. Paradoxically, it is at the isolated outposts where we are most different from others that we encounter the aspect of ourselves that is most the same—a genuine concern for the quality of our everyday lives.

How would we express genuine involvement in everyday living? What does it take to be fully alive? An answer was given when a disciple was asked, "What was most important to your teacher?" He replied, "Whatever he happened to be doing at the moment."[4]

I cannot teach you the ten principles for making the most of everyday life, but "a little child and a thief can show you what they are":

From the child you can learn three things:
He is merry for no particular reason;

Never for a moment is he idle;
When he needs something, he demands it
vigorously.

The thief can instruct you in seven things:
He does his service by night;
If he does not finish what he has set out to do
in one night, he devotes the next night to it;
He and those who work with him, love one
another;
He risks his life for slight gains;
What he takes has so little value for him, that
he gives it up for a very small coin;
He endures blows and hardship, and it matters
nothing to him;
He likes his trade and would not exchange it for
any other.[5]

Paradoxically, we cannot begin to claim all the joy of everyday life without first accepting the sorrow. When a crisis occurs, we must be ready to make the most of it.

To prepare ourselves for these opportunities for transformation, we must remember that there are two kinds of sorrow and two kinds of joy. When a person broods over misfortunes by cowering in a corner and despairs of help—that fussing is a useless sort of sorrow. The other kind of sorrow is the honest grief of someone who accepts these losses and moves on to other experiences.

The same is true of joy. Some people escape into superficial pleasures to avoid both feeling the emptiness and undertaking the soul searching needed to fill the void. This is hollow joy. But a person who is truly joyful is like someone whose house has burned down: He feels a need deep in the soul and begins to build anew. Over every stone that is laid, the heart rejoices.[6]

For me, the turning point came when I faced the prospect of my death. This pivotal crisis allowed me to reorder my priorities in ways that have made me experience my life more fully. To make this transformation, I had to wander lost and alone for a time while I searched my soul to find out who I truly am. If I hadn't endured the holy insecurity of that lonely exploration, I wouldn't have been able to establish the ground where I now stand and feel at home—the place that is truly my own.

After I suffered the isolation of withdrawing into myself, I was able to return to the place from which I had started, as if for the first time. Like blind Art Tatum, I could see that the music I wanted to play was a song of my own particular place among the people I love.

2

Accepting Our Weaknesses Frees Our Strengths

❧ A tale is told of a deaf man who went walking past a place where a wedding festival was being held. The musicians sat off in a corner playing their instruments, while the guests danced merrily to the joyful music that filled the house.

The deaf man looked in through the window. The musicians were hidden from his view and all he could see were the wedding guests whirling about the room. Because he couldn't hear the music, the man concluded that the house was filled with madmen. He rushed off to warn the other members of the community to avoid them.[1]

During periods of personal and spiritual transformation, we dance to our own music that other people cannot hear. This is particularly true when we are undergoing an internal crisis of such intensity that others cannot imagine the disorientation we are experiencing. Often this means that we abandon many of the usual social standards by which attitudes and behavior are conventionally judged to be proper, nice, right, or even sane. Other people may not notice that we are undergoing these transformations, but to make the most of them, we must be willing to risk that they may see us as mad dancers.

Unless we are willing to withdraw from our present social context for a while, we won't be able to sort out *who we really are* from *who we are expected to be*. We may feel uncomfortable about the isolation from other people that occurs while we are exploring our own particular peculiarities, but the separation need only be temporary. Adolescence is an apt example. The teenager must make a clean break with the parents' values to return home someday as a person in his or her own right. The transformation is painful for everyone concerned, but the attachment must be broken if an adult-to-adult connection is ever to be made.

During those difficult years, one of my sons complained to me that his friends thought I was "cool." He told me that I didn't understand how difficult I was making it for him to get through the phase when teenagers need to see their parents as "jerks."

Personal transformations follow spiraling paths. We start out seeing ourselves as others see us, withdraw to discover who we truly are, and then return to where we started from. When we come home, we see clearly where we stand—as if for the first time.

I remember my own uneasiness when as an adult, I went through a kind of transformation that took these twists and turns. Throughout my adolescence and well into my twenties, I never knew the right thing to say to other people. I doggedly depended on my intellectual ability to compensate for my social ineptitude.

When ill at ease at a party, I offered minilectures on esoteric philosophy. I could never get myself to make other people comfortable by making small talk about popular, familiar topics. At the time, I imagined myself a fascinating character. In retrospect, I realize that the other seemingly interested guests were probably politely ignoring my arrogance.

When I had some success, my true self experienced it as a fragile facade that could barely mask the inner emptiness of how inadequate I actually felt. Family, friends, and cultural messages had all made clear that my worth was to be measured by how well I got along with other people—no matter how poorly I was getting along with myself.

When I judged myself according to their standards, I usually concluded I was a failure. Even at those odd times when, somehow or other, I managed to behave in a socially acceptable manner, privately I always felt, like a freak. I might be able to fool other people into believing that I was a regular person, but I felt that I was unfit for human company.

Almost everyone else understood how to relate appropriately to other people, but I just couldn't get the hang of it. I had a few friends—all social misfits like me. Although they were very bright, none of them finished school. Few could hold a job very long and none of them was popular with more "conventional" people.

Some of these other outcasts ended up in jail or in mental hospitals. Others lived in drugged hazes and died of overdoses. I saw myself as equally peculiar and I expected my own identity would also end up permanently spoiled. I could not envision that I might ever become both comfortable with myself and acceptable to some other people.

In retrospect, I realize that my transformation was gradual. While it was happening, I experienced the change as a sudden, unexpected collision with the outside world. It was as if I'd demolished a barrier I hadn't known was in my way.

My social problems reached a crisis point when my intellect could no longer compensate for my difficulty in relating to other people. When I was drafted into the army, I had to interrupt my graduate studies in psychology for two years. After I returned to school as a civilian, it took me many months to get back in gear with academic life.

I had completed my basic course work before being drafted and was to take my oral comprehensive examination after being discharged from the service. Because of that long delay, I had to study intensively for many months to prepare for the exam.

When I approached the examination room, I felt confident that I had once again mastered the materials I was expected to know, but I felt nervous about meeting with the examiners.

There had been so much turnover in the faculty while I was away that the only examiner with whom I had ever actually studied was the chairperson. I had gleaned what information I could about the others by reading their publications and listening to graduate-student gossip.

I showed up exactly on time, only to be told that there

would be a half hour delay during which I was to wait in the hallway outside of the examination room. By the time I was called back in, I had grown so tense and panicky that whatever confidence I'd felt earlier had dissipated. Reacting to the increased stress, my blood pressure rose too high for my chronically fragile nasal membranes to contain. As I sat down to face the board, my nose began to bleed profusely.

This symptom seemed completely out of place in the proper, dignified mood maintained by the examiners, my academic adversaries. I felt a desperate need to regain my composure and to restore social contact. With characteristic miscalculation, I tried to be funny by telling these somber authorities that having a nosebleed was my unconscious way of asking, "What does a guy have to do to pass this examination—bleed to death?" Not a single one of them even smiled!

From then on, it was all downhill. As each unfamiliar professor asked me a question, I gave an answer I hoped would conform with his or her academic orientation. It soon became clear to me that I was *not* doing well, but I stumbled forward as best I could.

After about an hour of interrogation, the board asked me to wait outside while they decided whether or not I had passed the examination. Ten minutes later, the chairperson came out to tell me their verdict—I had not failed, but neither had I passed. The examiners had concluded that even though they thought I knew the material, I hadn't answered their questions well enough for them to pass me this time. They granted me a six-month continuance during which I was to work on learning to express more clearly whatever knowledge I wanted to communicate.

The chairperson was reassuring about my chances of passing the next time I took the examination. She said, "I'm certain that you've studied the literature and understand the concepts. Your problem was that you were so anxious to say the right thing to each of the professors, you often got in your own way. Use these next six months to review the materials and work on developing more detachment. When you are reexamined, try to forget about pleasing the examiners. Just answer each question as if it came out of a black box."

During the following half year, I resumed studying for my next shot at the exam. I also made a conscious attempt to discover a path around my personal awkwardness, other than *thinking* my way through social situations. I tried analyzing away my tendency to say things that upset other people, but it seemed like an unsolvable problem. Intellectual acrobatics didn't work and trying to will myself to improve socially only made matters worse.

After a while, I gave up in despair. Once I surrendered to being stuck in this crisis, my transformation dreams began. The pivotal dream in the series began in a country club where I stood uncomfortable and alone amid a relaxed and chatty crowd. It seemed excruciatingly evident that I didn't fit in. When I attempted to move toward an exit, the other members blocked my way and insisted that no one was allowed to leave the grounds. I told them that I didn't have to follow their silly rules and that I would find some other place that was more to my liking.

I tore up my membership card and bolted out the clubhouse door. Once outside, I found myself in a valley surrounded on all sides by high mountains and empty of anything other than the ornate grounds of the clubhouse from which I had just escaped. In hope of finding a more suitable club, I decided to climb up out of the valley.

Partway up the mountainside, I came upon a hermit standing at the entrance to a cave. When I tried to get him to tell me how long a climb it was to the top, he asked me where I was headed. I told him I had just escaped from the country club in the valley and that I wanted to get to the other side of the mountain.

The old man laughed and said, "If you close your eyes, you'll see that *this is the other side of the mountain*." With my eyes closed, I turned back toward the valley and found that the manicured grounds of the country club had been transformed into a wonderland of forests, fields, and streams.

When I reviewed the dream the next day, I understood that each image represented a part of myself—the club was my constricting wish to fit in, the escape was my self-defeating defiance, the hermit was the wisdom I might acquire by attending to my isolation and to the towering mountains of my arrogance. Discerning what was the other side of the mountain depended on where I stood. For me it also stood for the flip side of my conflict between introversion and extroversion.

Up to that point in my life, I had considered myself a *flawed extrovert*. People, I thought, were supposed to be extroverts, so I saw myself as a failure at that. These dreams helped me to discover an option I hadn't considered: Not everyone is an extrovert—or should be. I could relax and allow myself to be the *consummate introvert* I truly am.

For a short time, I continued to accept occasional invitations to parties. Whenever I did, I always ate enough salted nuts to whet my thirst and then, after two or three martinis, I found myself socializing with strangers, exchanging small talk and telling stories. This pose seemed to satisfy my aspiration to be a successful extrovert, but I realized that it was never really any fun for me. The morning after, inevitably I awoke with a bellyache from the peanuts, a hangover from the martinis, a belly full of socializing, and a resolution to avoid future parties.

I gave up party going altogether. At first I misunderstood my newly claimed introversion, thinking that I would only be happy as a recluse who lived alone inside his head. For a time, I withdrew into myself and rarely spoke to anyone else. The isolation was painfully lonely.

Gradually, I realized that much of the time what goes on in my own imagination fascinates me more than most of the people and events in the world around me, so I needed a good bit of quiet time alone reading, writing, meditating, and listening to music. However, I also realized that I wanted to be myself with a few close friends. Although I still feel awkward about conventional social interactions, I'm better able to make intimate, one-on-one personal contacts.

I remain uncomfortable when I'm in a social context that calls for my acting formal and polite, but I am more accepting of my avoidance of casual social gatherings with people I scarcely know. When other people I value are willing to be personal and playful, I'm pleased to spend time with them. If they don't want to play, I'd rather go off and enjoy my solitude.

I cannot be myself in ways that work with most other people, but how many friends do I need? After accepting that I experience awkwardness when I'm trying to be somebody other than who I am, I have also come to accept the fact that my introversion means many people experience me as difficult to get along with. Fortunately, a few find that aspect of me acceptable or tolerable enough for us to have a relaxed relationship, free of the tension of pretense.

I enjoy the free play of intimacy within these selected relationships and I'm no longer willing to put up with the multitude of ceremonial social exchanges that once cluttered my life. Other than taking care of practical necessities such as banking and home repair, I avoid formal encounters altogether. My relationships with my immediate family, with a few close friends, and with my patients satisfy my need for personal contact with other people. Even those few cherished exchanges occasionally feel like overexposure and I'm left feeling peopled-out.

A tale is told of a guest who asked his host why his curtains were closed. "If you want people to look in, then why the curtains? And if you don't want them to look in, why the window?" The host replied, "When I want something to look in, I draw aside the curtains."[2]

The way I do therapy also reflects this acceptance of my introversion. I never take on anyone as a patient unless he or she seems like someone with whom I would find it personally meaningful to spend my time. We get to know one another by revealing ourselves directly without the social gloss of ceremonial small talk. We accomplish our professional therapeutic work within the fantasy playground of our personal relationship.

My own personal transformations such as the one I've just described have taken many different turns. Every transition has evolved slowly. I expect change to continue throughout my lifetime, distilling out the so-called impurities, leaving me with less of what others expect me to be and more of who I really am. My work on myself cannot be completed in one lifetime.

If we wish to change, becoming who we truly are, we must learn to rely on our own personal standards. A tale is told about a teacher named Zusya and his disciples. The disciples asked their teacher, "Why do you teach in this way when Moses taught in another way?"

"When I get to the coming world," the teacher replied, "there they will not ask me, 'Why were you not more like Moses?' Instead they will want to know, 'Why were you not more like Zusya?' "[3]

3

Sometimes Our True Selves Don't Fit Other People's Images of Who We Should Be

❧ A tale is told of a merchant named Sannyasin who inherited a large sum of family money.[1] He sold his shop, bought a big house that stood beside a temple, and spent his days studying the scriptures. The only irritant in the self-appointed, holy man's otherwise peaceful and pious life was Shudra, a poor street sweeper who had rented a rundown cottage across the road from Sannyasin's magnificent mansion.

When the wealthy man watched from the window of his study, he often saw Shudra returning home drunk after a hard day's work. Evening wine was all the poor man had to ease his difficult and unhappy life. Although he tried and tried to stop drinking, at the end of each miserable and exhausting day, Shudra got drunk again. On the following morning, he always felt truly sorry about having indulged himself the previous night and prayed that God would forgive him.

One evening, the holy man called out to the sweeper, "How can you live like that? If you don't change your ways, you will be punished for your sins in the next life." Although his wealthy neighbor's admonition made Shudra feel guilty, he continued to get drunk. Because his advice did not discourage Shudra's misbehavior, Sannyasin became so upset with the sweeper that he began to keep count of his sins by setting aside a small stone each time he caught the poor man coming home drunk.

After several weeks of tallying Shudra's faults, Sannyasin called out to him, "See this pile of pebbles! Each stone stands for a time you got drunk, even after I had warned you that continuing your evil ways would damn you to an eternity in Hell." Trembling at the sight of the stones that reflected the accumulation of his sins, the wretched sweeper implored God to save him from the miserable life he had.

When the Lord heard Shudra's prayers, He sent the angel of death to rescue him from his misery. That same day, Sannyasin also died.

Heaven's envoys descended to lift Shudra's spirit to the place of eternal peace. At the same moment, the emissaries of the underworld arose to drag Sannyasin's soul down to hell. Both men were astounded.

The grateful street sweeper remained silent while the outraged holy man cried out to God, "You call this justice? I spent my life immersed in the sacred scriptures, and am damned to Hell, while that drunk whose sins I've counted is going to Heaven!"

God's messengers answered, "You spent your days admiring your own image. The Lord is sending you to Hell so that you can see more clearly just what sort of soul you have. Shudra sinned, but his honest attempts to stop drinking showed an openness of heart. Your vain absorption in counting *his* sins revealed the impurities hidden in your own heart. Your intoxication with vanity shows that it is really *you*, not Shudra, who is the drunken sinner."

Like Sannyasin, many of us want to believe that we are special, that our efforts to be good are better than someone else's. Few of us are as willing as Shudra was to openly reveal our struggles with our personal weaknesses. Most of us have an urgent desire to appear normal and nice, but we cannot maintain these idealized images of ourselves without denying, even to ourselves, the parts of who we truly are that don't fit the way we'd like to be seen.

When we attempt to hide whatever we imagine might appear eccentric or weird, we also risk obscuring the richness of any exceptional aspects of who we are. *We each have something precious in us that does not exist in anyone else.* The universal human possibilities are uniquely combined in each particular person. The colorfulness of our individual personalities shows up clearly when we carefully observe which way our own hearts draw us and then choose to walk this personal path with all our strength. The true value of our accomplishments is that we each bring them about *in our own way and by our own efforts*.

The underside of the singular glory in each of our souls is the base perversity that is its dark twin. The higher power that exists in every soul can only be evoked when we are also willing to call forth the demons within us that are pitted against its emergence. Becoming the best person we can be requires that we accept the worst in us as well.

Only by setting aside our idealized image of who we imagine we should be, can we allow the emergence of that awkward combination of strength and weakness that is our true self. The tension between the creative and destructive, light and dark, holy and horrible, generates the energy required to propel our growth and development. We all struggle with these inner contradictions, each in his or her own way.

Both spiritual and personal growth are individual attainments. As Martin Buber notes, what kind of God would make us all so different and then allow only one way to serve Him?[2]

When we honor our peculiarities, the process of personal transformation allows us to become all that we might be.[3] Making the most of our differences sounds simple, but it isn't easy. If we deviate very far from the norm, even in our physical appearances, most of us feel uncomfortable.

For centuries it was socially unacceptable to be too tall or too short, too thin or too fat, or to make other people uncertain about the extent of our individuality, or the nature of our sexuality. Those who "challenged the conventional boundaries between male and female, sexed and sexless, animal and human, large and small, self and other,"[4] were banished as outcasts or, as in previous eras, displayed in freak shows as Giants and Dwarfs, Fat Ladies and Living Skeletons, as Siamese Twins, or as Hermaphrodites.

Since the 1960s, we have seen the young of each generation challenge the conventional norms of their parents by flaunting androgyny and other defiant displays of deviance intended to subvert traditional authority and assert individual freedom. Phase-appropriate flamboyance is the necessary developmental transition of young people, aimed at evolving identities of their own. But adolescent rebellion is a misleading model for the eventual individual adult development of a true self.

Ironically, in trying to be different from their parents, teenagers turn out to be lookalikes of each other. What starts out as a quest for freedom to be and do as each adolescent pleases ends up as a cultlike compliance to fads. These attempts at individuality are undermined even more when fashion designers and other trend setters legitimize youthful deviance by transforming anomalies into stylish norms for the older generation whom they were originally intended to defy.

Like the earlier popularity of freak shows, our adult fascination with adolescent aberrations reflects a need to reassure ourselves that we are neither too big nor too small nor in any way peculiar—that *we are just right*. The odd creatures on display reassure us that *they are the freaks and we are not*.

The most obvious oddities with whom we avoid being categorized are *physical* freaks. However, we also see *moral* and *social* deviance as stigmata of spoiled identities. The conventional wisdom we call conscience encourages us to deny that we all have evil urges.

The legend of the breaking of the vessels recounted in the Prologue teaches that the divine sparks dwell everywhere, even in our wrongdoings. This means that we cannot claim to be in touch with our inner power unless we recognize and acknowledge our hidden weaknesses. Buber asserts that "God loves the wicked people who know that they are wicked more than the righteous ones who know that they are righteous."[5]

When we pretend that we have no awful aspects of our own, we risk two unfortunate consequences: (1) we often project onto others whatever we disown in ourselves and (2) unwittingly, we act out the unacceptable thoughts and feelings that we consciously intend to keep hidden.

As an example of the first point, when I find myself offended by the self-righteousness I see in others, I am reacting to the pietism and arrogance I so often deny in myself. Ironically, at the same time, when I presume that it is my place to judge their character, I unwittingly display the inflated piousness that I am trying to deny as part of my own imperfect self.

The second negative consequence of denying our own dark sides is that, unless we are willing to bring our peculiarities out of the shadows into light, we cannot expect to remain safe from their unexpected exposure. Hiding our weaknesses requires that we use precious energy standing guard to protect ourselves against all that we might openly reveal. Still, as carefully as we watch, we will sometimes be caught off guard. To not waste energy trying to avoid the inevitable, we must claim as our own all our imperfections, even though we prefer to pretend these only exist in other people.

Evil urges are not the only parts of ourselves that we are tempted to shunt off into the darkness. Our *shadow side*, according to Carl Jung, includes any aspect of ourselves that we consider "merely somewhat inferior, primitive, unadapted, and awkward; not wholly bad. It contains undeveloped, childish, or primitive qualities which would in a way vitalize and embellish human existence."[6]

The core of each of our personalities is a primordial

chaos of contradictions—good and evil, weakness and strength, brutality and compassion—all that is sacred and all that is profane. We claim some aspects of this core as our public image. In hiding whatever else we are from ourselves and others, we create our shadow side. And in the act of hiding, we reinforce our sense of being lost and alone.

In some of us, hidden in our shadow sides are worthwhile parts of ourselves that we can't comfortably claim. These are our "bright shadows." For example, my earliest image of myself was that of a bad child. Whenever I tried to behave in a way that I hoped would please my parents, my mother would say, "Look how that bad boy tries to pretend he's good."

Eventually, I began to believe that being bad was the only thing I was any good at. All of my attempts to be a decent person seemed like exercises in futility. Eventually, in despair, I began to actively pursue the evil urge, hoping that at least I might achieve the status of an outstanding delinquent.

Eventually, I learned to lie more easily than I told the truth, to express irreverence more readily than respect, and to seek vengeance rather than forgive an offense. I tried my hand at cheating and stealing, and learned to savor a smorgasbord of forbidden fruits such as drugs, sexual deviance, streetwise hustling, and almost automatic defiance of authority.

Convinced that I was by nature wild and crazy, I became contemptuous of whatever I interpreted as the self-righteousness of sane, well-behaved, conventional people. I avoided the straight-arrow civilized world, became fascinated with the seamy side of life, and sought out other misfits, like myself, who were drawn to perversity.

The dark shadow of evil and madness has always been easier for me to accept than the *bright shadow* of well-mannered conformity and considerate appreciation of other people's standards of good conduct. I feared that the softer side of myself would make me vulnerable to some secret slavish devotion to pleasing anyone who might make the mistake of finding me acceptable.

I remember clearly, but rarely without feeling tearful, a quiet conversation that occurred in an early romantic relationship. As I became aware that the young woman and I were becoming committed to one another, I felt obliged to warn her that I was an emotionally unstable, hostile person who mistreated everyone I met. I was touched and astonished when she answered, "We've spent a good deal of time together and you haven't ever hurt me."

It was then that I began trying to become aware of all that was hidden in my own bright shadow. So far, it has turned out to be the least successful of my attempts at personal growth, but I'm still working on it. I remain uncomfortable when someone whom I value sees me as a good soul. I've never had a completely pure impulse in my life. A single lifetime is too short to complete some transformations.

Because fashions change and social standards shift, I cannot always count on remaining a maverick. I still feel embarrassed whenever some aspect of my eccentricity becomes congruent with a current trend. For example, when the encounter group ethic of obligatory "sharing" of socially unacceptable feelings came into vogue in the 1970s, at least temporarily my idiosyncratic outspokenness had become a popular mode of behavior.

Some of the crises in our lives may be as monumental

as facing a life-threatening illness, as I described in chapter 1. Other crises are simply a buildup of minor incidents, with one last straw catching us off guard and making us feel unprepared.

For example, I remain so ill at ease with people I meet on a casual basis that even a collection of minor mishaps can make me act like a madman. I end up projecting my own extreme discomfort onto people I hardly know. A recent incident occurred when I had several errands that required dealing with brief acquaintances and total strangers. As a way of getting these uncomfortable encounters over with, I made the mistake of trying to do all the chores on the same morning. Why can't I learn that this tactic doesn't work for me?

I began by going to pick up a new hearing aid. The technician was decent and accommodating, but just as I was ready to leave he began to talk. He apologized for the delay in filling my order, explaining that he'd become ill on the plane coming home from his vacation.

My uneasiness was growing but since I can empathize with sudden illness, I responded sympathetically, acknowledging how frightening the crisis must have been for him. These comments encouraged him to continue, but by then my anxiety began to take over. As he boasted that he would have gotten along fine on his own, but he'd been traveling with his wife, and her concern had simply made him feel worse, I interrupted our talk by abruptly leaving his office.

From there, I drove to a shopping mall—the sort of public place I usually avoid. The only reason I ventured there was I urgently needed a new coffee maker. The first store I tried no longer carried the kind I wanted. The unsuspecting sales clerk further irritated my quickly fraying nerves when he offered irrelevant information. Discomfort got the best of me again, so I turned away abruptly and left him, too.

Making my way through crowds in malls isn't physically easy for me. So, by the time I'd purchased an acceptable alternative at another store, I was so unsettled I couldn't remember where I'd parked my car. When I finally found it, I discovered I was no longer carrying the package with my hearing aid. Too rattled to go back and search, I gave up any hope of trying to find it and drove back to my office as fast as possible.

In the end, my package was recovered through the lost-and-found office at the mall. Nevertheless, the incidents were distressing because I had brought the whole fiasco on myself. Trying to do too much at once—knowing those were chores I don't like and don't handle well—I made a general mess of things and made myself miserable while I was at it.

In retrospect, I'm amused at just how crazy I still can get. I have solved some of my personality problems. Others surface less often and when one does, the exposure doesn't last as long or hurt as much as it once did. There are some problems that I'll never solve, and some I won't bother to try.

Each of us goes through times when our efforts to be our true selves get stalled or go awry. This episode reflects one of the present limitations to my own personal and spiritual growth. At times, my residual stubbornness invites misadventures that leave me feeling even more lost and alone than before I started searching for my true self. The self I see as most truly me is unsuited for dealing with some situations. When and if I'm ever ready to tackle one of those, I'll get on with it. In the meantime, I must suffer the absurdities I bring on myself.

We cannot control personal changes by acts of will or accomplish much without doing whatever it takes to see something through. However, to optimize our chances of succeeding, we must not only understand the satisfactions our peculiarities afford us but also accept the price we pay for indulging them. I'm now able to do this more often than I once was, but I still have a long way to go.

Obsessing about ourselves is not enough. Buber notes, "You can rake the muck this way, rake the muck that way—it will always be muck. Have I sinned or have I not sinned? In the time I am brooding over it, I could be stringing pearls for the delight of Heaven."[7]

4

When We Are Lost, We Must Find Our Own Way Home

❧ A tale is told of a young woman who went to the wisest man in her village and tearfully told him that after a dozen years of marriage, she'd not yet been able to have a baby.[1] When he asked what she was willing to do about it, the young woman did not know how to answer him.

The wise man told her, "Before I was born my own aging mother had not yet had a child. She went to see a holy man who had stopped off at an inn in her village and begged him to pray for her. When the holy man asked her what she was willing to do about it, she explained that although she and her husband were poor, they did own one thing of value that she would bring to him.

"My mother hurried home and got out the one good cape she'd stowed away in a chest, but by the time she got back to the inn, the holy man had already left. She set out after him without any money, and so she had to walk from town to town carrying her cape.

"When my mother finally caught up with the holy man, he accepted the cape, hung it up on the wall and told her that all would be well. My mother walked all the way back home. A year later, I was born."

The young woman answered that like the wise man's mother, she would bring a cape so that she too could bear a child. The wise man replied, "That won't work. You heard my story. My mother had no tale to go by. Like her, you'll need to create your own story."

When we've reached a dead end during a crisis, other people's experiences can serve as models for getting unstuck and going forward again, but the only way we can learn and grow from the obstacles we encounter is to find our own answers and work through our difficulties in our own way.

The young woman's struggle reminds me of a crisis I was only able to resolve by creating my own story. It was a career crisis that would have resulted in total burnout, if I hadn't discovered how to transform my professional life into a personal experience.

Some of us devote our working lives to careers that start out promising to be both worthwhile and satisfying. After a while, most of us discover that the path we have chosen has not led us where we hoped it would. We experience the shattering of our idealized expectations as the despair of burnout.

At that point, many people settle for a disappointing work life, cynically concluding, "At least it's a living." A few give up and turn to some other vocation, often to find that they are only repeating the same unsatisfying cycle, listlessly wondering why life hasn't treated them fairly. Some people choose to deny the conflict between their early ideals and what their work later turns out to be, ignoring the fact that they are not serving others well and insisting what they are doing remains a dedicated, noble undertaking.

Career crises can be painful, but they also offer opportunities to change our lives for the better. For example, people who get fired may, as a result of being forced to find new jobs, discover work that is far more fulfilling than their previous jobs. Those who are desperately dissatisfied may quit what they're doing, give up a career in progress and start all over again to find work they value. Others may face crises within their professions that transform their work into an experience more fulfilling than they'd ever envisioned.

It took me almost ten years to arrive at the critical crossroads in my own career. I now regret the time I wasted playing it safe by following paths chosen by my mentors instead of risking what it took to find my own direction— all the while refusing to recognize how increasingly empty of passion my efforts had become.

In retrospect, I can see that I was headed for a fall from the start because I trusted what other people told me more than I trusted my own feelings. By the time I entered college, I'd already felt like a misfit for a long time. I had chosen to pursue a career as a psychotherapist, hoping that my own personal anguish would allow me to understand and help people with similar problems.

My college psychology professors encouraged me to view troubled souls as subjects in experiments aimed at reshaping their maladaptive habit patterns. In graduate school, I was taught a more psychoanalytic orientation.

The first mistake led me to try to develop an attitude of scientific detachment toward my patients. The second encouraged my taking on an impersonal attitude by presenting a blank screen onto which their transferences could be projected.

Neither role seemed to suit either me or my patients. While completing my training, I worked in correctional, psychiatric, and military institutions with involuntary patients who were pretty much stuck with accepting what little I had to offer.

Finally, with doctorate in hand, I went to work at a community mental health center that the staff called "the ghetto clinic." Today it would be "an inner-city resource." Most of the poor, black patients showed up late for their appointments. It took me a while to figure out that they didn't come on time because they usually had to wait hours for public health services.

I began treating a young, unhappy, semiliterate, single parent—a second-generation welfare mother who'd been raised in an impoverished broken home. Her baby had been bitten by a rat and developed an infection that the doctors couldn't seem to cure.

She came to the clinic complaining of irritability and depression. I stumbled around for several sessions silently formulating interpretations of her problem without ever making any real personal contact with her. Foolishly, I hypothesized that her moodiness was simply a reaction to having been abandoned as a child and having remained trapped in poverty. If only I could help her to evolve the right attitude for developing marketable skills, I was sure that her symptoms would be eased. I made the mistake of explaining all of this to her and patronizingly assured her, "I understand how you feel."

She became enraged and shouted, "You don't understand shit! What would a honky head doctor know about getting hurt—high, wide, and frequently?" She went on to tell me, "I got the blues because my baby is dying and you tell me I'm depressed because I'm an ignorant black woman who can't get a job. Blues ain't where you been or where you going. Blues is where you are!"

Taken off guard, I interpreted her "negative overreaction," as displaced anger toward the father who deserted her. It was the end of the hour and so before she could reply, I announced, "We can talk about it the next time we meet. Right now our time is up."

Before slamming the office door on her way out, she turned to me and mocked, "*Our time*, my ass! That's just shrink talk. It's *my* time. You act like it's *your* time. And then you call it *our* time." I knew I'd screwed up, but I didn't understand just what I'd done wrong.

Following my unexpected clash with that welfare mother, I could no longer explain away the guilt and helplessness I'd tried to deny for so long. That night I had a peculiarly abstract dream in which I watched a kaleidoscopic display of many small black dots and one large white one. I watched them move as if directed toward some intended design, but they always ended up in a seemingly random arrangement.

The next morning, I pondered the meaning of my dream, hoping that if only I could accurately interpret it, I would understand what had gone wrong in the therapy. First, I thought that the answer lay in the *color* of the dots—that the problem was my lack of understanding of my black patients.

When that didn't feel right, I focused on the differences in the *size* of the dots. I tried to believe that I had trouble identifying with my poor and powerless patients because I had education, money, and position while they had to do without. When that interpretation didn't help any more than the first, I gave up trying to analyze the dream.

Later that afternoon, I talked with my clinical supervisor about the previous day's disastrous therapy session. Unexpectedly, I found myself adding two previously overlooked details: My patient always seemed unable to remember my name and, now, I had forgotten hers.

All at once, I understood the core meaning of the previous night's dream. It was not the color or the size of the images so much as their *abstract* quality. I realized that the trouble with my work as a therapist was that for years I'd been approaching patients in an impersonal way—as if we were merely dots that had to be properly repatterned.

I wasn't at all sure that my patient would come back for her next appointment. She did show up, mainly because she had more anger to express, and partly because she wanted to find out what the Hell was wrong with me. Uncharacteristically, I told her that I thought she was right to feel angry and I apologized for having treated her so impersonally. For the first time, I felt genuine empathy for her helplessness about the pain and danger her precious baby was suffering.

To my astonishment, I found myself telling her about the birth of my oldest son. He'd been born with a life-threatening, congenital deformity that had required immediate surgery. I spoke of how unprepared I'd felt to face that misfortune and described the weeks I'd spent helplessly sitting beside his incubator, unable even to hold him—much less to help him. To my amazement, I began to cry.

I tried to reassure myself by telling my patient that all of this had happened many years ago and that my son had grown up to live a full and healthy life. She interrupted my flight from what was left of my grief and helplessness by saying, "It has to hurt to remember a time you couldn't do shit to save your own child." And then she too began crying.

In the past, there had been rare instances when I had exposed some personal weakness in front of a patient. This was the first time I'd revealed anything personal about myself in response to a patient's vulnerability. I wasn't crying in front of her, or she in front of me. We were crying *together*.

My tears felt right at the time, but afterward I worried about having acted out in a way I'd been taught to consider unprofessional. I told my supervisor about what had gone on and of my worry that it might not have served my patient well. All he said was, "She'll never forget what happened—and neither will you. Try to trust yourself."

A wise man once said, "The teacher helps his disciples to find themselves, but in hours of desolation, it is the disciples who help the teacher to find himself again."[2] After my experience with this young woman, my attitude toward my patients was never the same. I returned to the clinic feeling passionate about my work, but in a new way.

The therapy I've done since that transformation has evolved from an impersonal rearrangement of abstract patterns into a lively dialogue between two vulnerable human beings. The patient tells me his or her story and I tell mine. In this intimate atmosphere, the work gets done within the personal context of our evolving relationship.

Meeting as two people who are soulfully dedicated to sharing their real selves, each releasing divine sparks, creates the intimacy and warmth needed for the personal growth of both of us. My disclosures don't teach my patients how to live, and what they tell me doesn't determine what I do. We each must find our own way, but the openness and caring of intimate companions makes being on our own easier to bear.

5

Learning to Listen with Your Heart

❧ A religious leader was sitting by the side of a road with many members of his congregation gathered around him when, all at once, he felt that he had to tell them a certain funny story he'd once heard. Because it wasn't the sort of reverent spiritual tale that he usually shared with his flock, he feared that the earthy joke that was on his mind would cause criticism. He worried that they might no longer consider him worthy of their devotion, but in his heart he believed that all joys come from Heaven—even a joke, if it is offered with heartfelt joy.

Setting aside how seriously he usually took his role as religious leader, he went ahead and told the story. The people around him burst out laughing. From then on, those members of his congregation who had doubted his spiritual leadership became devoted to him.[1]

Often the most rewarding things we do come about not

because we have a great idea, but because we respond to our feelings. These treasures and times of great value are rare, but they are most likely to happen when we listen to our hearts. That's certainly the way it's always worked for me.

Soon after I learned to read, I dreamed secretly that someday I might become a writer. I tried writing some short stories when I was still a kid, but my teachers and my parents so often told me I was going about it the wrong way that soon I stopped trying. As an adolescent, I scribbled some surrealistic fragments I imagined might someday be expanded into works worth reading, but I was too shy to show them to anyone and too scared of failure to complete them.

I loved to read books that other people had written because they filled my imagination with worlds more satisfying than the one I lived in. Early on, I learned to tell colorful stories because I believed that otherwise no one would be interested in what I had to say.

It was not until I reached my thirties that I settled down to do some serious writing. After I'd completed my dissertation, I wanted to write about all I'd experienced as a young therapist. I'd had a couple of pieces published in professional journals that I believed some people might find useful to read, but they were no fun to write.

I loved reading poetry but I had no talent for creating it, so instead I set out to write a novel. After a couple of years of labored effort, I accumulated a thick pile of manuscript pages. The quantity was reassuring, but the quality was discouraging.

Unwilling to face how inadequate this made me feel, I made excuses for my failings by complaining to my wife that I had too little free time to produce the wonderful novel I could otherwise have written. Shamelessly, I protested that it was the financial burden of supporting our family that stood in the way of my becoming a happily creative artist and commercially successful novelist. My wife answered, "If free time is what you need, quit your job. We'll find a way to manage."

I felt deeply touched by her response, but I was too terrified to put myself to the test. Some part of me secretly understood that I was unprepared to write a really good novel and unready to put in the years of work it might take for me to learn how.

When I faced up to those feelings, I despaired of ever succeeding as a writer. I talked with my wife about how discouraged I felt and tried to explore what form, if any, my creative efforts might take. There were all sorts of writing that seemed personally satisfying to their authors and commercially marketable to their audiences. I had begun to doubt that I had any talent for writing that could accommodate to any of the conventional forms.

My wife suggested that, for the time being, I forget about the form in which my work might be published and concentrate on writing what I felt in my heart. Up until then, I hadn't considered writing without worrying about who would read it or why, much less pay good money for something I'd written. It was astonishing to envision that I might devote myself to writing whatever I wished to express, simply for my own pleasure. *Transformations require that we let go of familiar ways of doing things, without yet knowing what we will do next.*

For a while, I tried writing short personal essays by drawing on spiritual literature that had long appealed to me, I described images of helpers, healers, and guides from long ago and faraway that served as metaphors for contemporary psychotherapists. Some of the pieces got published in an offbeat humanistic professional journal.[2]

As I pursued my writing, I gradually realized that I continued to gather metaphors reflecting how one person could help other people with their personal problems. Finally, feeling sufficiently encouraged by some of the responses to my brief personal pieces, I reconsidered writing a longer work. However, still too timid to attempt a book that would be all mine, I blocked out an anthology of other people's writings, woven around my own interest in metaphors for people to help one another.

A therapist friend who had a book of her own in press told her publisher about my idea, and a couple of weeks later he phoned to ask to see an outline. I was sufficiently delighted to set aside my fear of failure and put together a proposal for the anthology. I included a couple of my own recently published journal pieces in the packet I mailed to the publisher.

A few weeks later, he called to say he was interested in the anthology, but felt disappointed I wasn't considering writing a book of my own. As soon as I got off the phone, I realized that I too felt disappointed. Fifteen minutes later I called back to tell him I did want to write one of my own that would include the pieces he'd liked and promised to send him a new proposal.

It was toward the end of the time when I was writing that book[3] that I underwent my first bout of neurosurgery. That incapacitating ordeal required that I put off completing my manuscript, interrupt my work as a psychotherapist, and disrupt much of my everyday private life as well.

During my recuperation at home, I wrote a personal memoir about all I'd been through[4] intended primarily as a therapeutic effort to put my life back together and as a communication to friends and family. I also sent a copy to my publisher as an explanation of why I wasn't meeting the contractual deadline for completion of my manuscript. He wrote back immediately suggesting that we append the memoir as epilogue to the book. I agreed.

This was the beginning of the discovery of a personal style of writing that has since produced more than a dozen books. It is an odd admixture of autobiography, clinical experiences, and the legends, myths, folktales, and creative literature that had so long fascinated me as a reader.

I'm not aware of a particular name for this style of writing; it was enough that it began to make me feel more alive. Even though there were times when it added to my frustration, for the most part it felt like fun. As I continue, there are moments when writing drives me crazy, but my restlessness between books makes me realize that it is this same "craft or sullen art,"[5] as Dylan Thomas called it, that keeps me sane.

My wife helped edit my earliest writings, and then, to make room for her own efforts, she stopped completely. At first, I felt hurt. Then I got angry with her, even though she did remain responsive to how I felt about my writing. Eventually I became aware of how liberating it was to be able to write as I pleased without wondering what my wife or anyone else would think of what I had written.

After the first of my books had begun to sell well, I asked my wife how she felt about my continuing immersion in writing. She answered simply, "I'm glad it brings you so much joy." She seemed to have known all along what it took me so many years to discover.

Too often, we become caged by the rules we try to follow, whether we have them imposed on us by other people or we set them in place by ourselves. At times, we can only escape by attending to our personal feelings at the particular moment when we hear their call.

When we stand solidly on the earth, our heads reach up to Heaven. If we let the spiritual light penetrate the darkness of our souls until the darkness itself shines, we no longer need to separate our heads from our hearts. Our ability to do this lies in devoting ourselves completely to everything we do by responding with our whole being to the unique claim of singular situations.

I'm reminded of a man about whom I've written elsewhere.[6] I first met Salik long ago during one of my family's August vacations on Cape Cod. For years he had been a highly successful practicing psychoanalyst in New York City, as well as an unknown amateur Sunday painter. It was on a summer vacation of his own several years earlier that he confronted a crisis that transformed his life. Giving up the studied role assigned him by his Middle European Jewish upbringing, he took on a risky and exciting life of daily improvisation.

Salik had gone to Haiti for just three weeks. There he met a beautiful black butterfly of a woman who was an actress and a primitive painter. By the time the vacation was nearing an end, they knew that they had fallen in love. For a few days they played at planning to reunite someday soon. But Salik knew that if he left then, he would never return and that that would be the end of it.

Instead they decided to marry then and there. His wife returned to New York with him just long enough for Salik to close down his practice, to gather together what little money they each had, and to get on with redefining their lives by devoting themselves to the painting that was their passion.

They knew that they could not live very long on the little money they had and the bit more they might make. Salik told me that their working plan was to count on spending $4,000 a year for necessities, and another $4,000 on incidentals.

By the time we met, they'd been married for several years and had three exotically beautiful children. They were living for six months of the year in a house on Gull Pond on the Cape and the other six months in Cuernavaca, Mexico. When I expressed concern about the difficulty their children might have shifting back and forth each year from an English- to a Spanish-speaking country, Salik and his wife both laughed. It turned out that at home in the family, they all spoke French and played it by ear outside in whatever country they were in at the time.

Salik himself had become a satisfied, successful colorist. That summer my wife and I bought one of his large canvases—a powerful and intense mixture of dark mottled yellows and astonishing floods of red. It still hangs on our living room wall.

As we got to know each other better, Salik told me of the confusion among the other analysts he knew in response to his having switched roles. After living away from New York for a while, he began receiving recognition as an artist. His agent arranged a one-man show for him in a New York gallery. Salik made plans to return to help set up the show.

He contacted some of his ex-colleagues from his years

as a psychoanalyst. They were delighted to hear from him, arranged a dinner party in his honor, and offered to help him reopen his practice and return to being the person they knew him to be. Salik was grateful, but assured them that he was happy and successful as his true self by being an artist.

Only one of the other analysts ever contacted him again and did so to explain that they had only welcomed him back because, mistakenly, they were sure that he was returning because he had failed. He could only guess that his freedom to seize the moment and change his life must have posed too great a threat to their complacency about their own lives.

Salik's story illustrates that if we always play it safe, following the rule of reason, we are certain to miss out on our claim to tomorrow's treasures. However, when we turn toward new ways of knowing ourselves, we may encounter unexpected difficulties. Yet, if we are able to work these critical situations through, we will be astonished to discover how much is possible that was once unimaginable. Talents, goals, accomplishments we were afraid to dream of can become a natural part of who we are!

It's dangerous to undertake the search for the rewards to be found in personal transformations without understanding the risks that such quests inevitably entail. If we follow our hearts, we may find joy beyond belief, but the path is also scattered with fearful obstacles of uncertainty and isolation.

In learning to follow our hearts and live our own lives, we are certain to experience times when we feel lost and alone. Even though we may understand that God is close by, at times we will know the remoteness and the loneliness that occur when we are left entirely on our own and feel totally unprepared to decide what we must do next, but if we are willing to pursue paths that are true to ourselves, then somewhere along the way we will once again encounter the higher power within us. Meister Eckhart tells us that "the eye with which I see God is the same as that with which He sees me."[7]

To make my way through those troubled times of temporary separation from the God within my soul, while awaiting, I find it reassuring to think of Buber's description of the parent who sets out to teach a child to walk. The mother or father stands beckoning while holding one hand on either side to prevent the youngster from falling. The child moves toward the parent between these protecting hands.

But the moment the youngster comes close, the parent moves away a little with hands held farther apart. The loving parent does this over and over, so that the child may learn to stand and walk on his or her own feet.[8] In the same way, the crises in life challenge us to grow and we are faced with the critical choice of whether or not to trust our own inner power to meet that challenge in a way that is true to ourselves.

PART II

❧

Honoring Our Peculiarities as One Way of Finding the Higher Power Within Us

To be nobody but yourself in a world doing its best to make you everybody else means to fight the hardest battle any human can ever fight and never stop fighting.

—*e. e. cummings*

All of you is worth something, if you will only own it.

—*Sheldon Kopp*

Honoring Our Peculiarities
as One Way of Finding
the Higher Power within Us:
Introduction to Part II

Biographies are chronologies of crises—stories of people in conflict, often with themselves. The challenges others faced, the choices they made, and the consequences they suffered or enjoyed can be instructive to all of us. Some of the transformations we will examine have been drawn from the lives of pioneering soul searchers who have broken ground for the rest of us. These trailblazers have gone to the edge of good and evil, artistic freedom and domestic love, inner searching and worldly adventure. Their explorations map out landscapes that some of us have not yet entered.

Personal transformations don't always work out well. Some are creative times and lead to ecstasy. Others are catastrophic and end in unhappiness. The biographies we will be considering offer extreme examples of the rewards and the risks that come with the territory.

Some of the people I have chosen as examples succeeded brilliantly in making the most of the crises in which they found themselves caught. Each of these victorious individuals has been paired with a counterpart who failed dismally. These opposites to be contrasted are Jean-Paul Sartre and the Marquis de Sade, as two who tested the limits of personal freedom; Georgia O'Keeffe and Diane Arbus, both explorers of the edge of artistic independence; Malcolm X and Abbie Hoffman, who committed themselves to social causes; and Thomas Merton and Bhagwan Shree Rajneesh, both expanding the boundaries of spiritual exploration.

Most of us are neither as famous as the best of these guides, nor as notorious as the worst of them. Our successes are less glorious, and our failures less disastrous. The creative and destructive extremes of these polar pairs respectively offer inspiration and warning to those of us who undertake more modest transformations.

In these four chapters, along with each pair of well-known people who have gone to the edge in their exploration of personal growth, we will examine the experiences of a patient of mine who set out on a comparable course. In each case, my patient's life changes pivoted on a sequence of transformation dreams.

If we interpret dreams as our unconscious expression of yesterday's conflicts, we may learn more about how our problems began. However, if we learn to experience these nocturnal images as our soul's observations about today's crises, they can guide us to the place where tomorrow's personal growth will take us.[1]

6

We Are Free to Choose What Sort of Lives We Will Live

Many people believe that the best way to serve God is exemplified by the followers of traditional religion, that is those who affirm their spirituality by leading austere lives, devoted to studying sacred scriptures and immersing themselves in ritual prayer. The spiritual way that moves me most is both more mystical and more personal than this traditional approach.

It is the way of ordinary people leading active, everyday lives and honoring the higher power within themselves by meeting others lovingly. If we believe that God made us as we are "because He does not want people to be caged in their lusts, but to be free in them,"[1] we serve Him by engaging in earthly delights with heartfelt devotion.

Some of us simply conform to the constraints we accept as social reality and give up trying to bring more personal meaning to our lives. Others conform overtly, while covertly committing forbidden acts, and then they feel guilty. A few of us call into question how we live and seek greater freedom to grow into all we might be. *The freer we are, the more creative we can be; but increasing our freedom also expands our capacity for being destructive.*

Jean-Paul Sartre[2] and the Marquis de Sade[3] are polar extremes of the rewards and risks of the search for inner freedom. Although separated by several generations, both were raised as favored children of well-to-do French families. Both felt oppressed by the values that were imposed on them, but they extended the limits of their personal freedom to very different ends. Sartre won accolades as a successful philosophical and literary leader of his generation, while Sade is remembered as an imprisoned pornographer whose name became a synonym for a cruel sexual perversion.

World War II divided Sartre's life in two. The routine of the first part of his life was shattered when his career as an apolitical high-school philosophy teacher was disrupted by his conscription into the French army. First he lived as an anonymous soldier under military authority, next as an inmate of a Nazi prisoner-of-war camp, and then as an oppressed civilian during the German occupation of Paris. Sartre coped by undergoing a complete turnabout. He started out as a disengaged academic and ended up becoming a committed activist.

When Sartre saw that the validity of his academic theories could only be confirmed by actions in everyday life, he was reborn a new man, ready to plunge himself into "a worldwide political project of concrete action."[4] He became an influential world-class philosopher who attempted to unite the splintered antagonistic factions of his time.

Sartre was at odds within himself as well. He had internal conflicts to resolve—ends versus means, fervor versus discipline, and authentic personal goals versus artificial social expectations. He examined his experiences and searched his soul, trying to think and write his way out of both the internal contradictions of everything he'd been taught to believe in, and the arbitrary restrictions of social conduct that had been imposed on him.

In part, his existential philosophy emerged out of attempts to extricate his true self from the oppressive constraints that had defined his life. Gradually, he recognized that we are all born into families and cultures we didn't choose, given names we didn't pick, instructed in behavior and values we might not have freely chosen, and that too often we end up expected to live lives designed by others.

Once Sartre realized that his own assigned identity had no authentic personal meaning, he understood that we all have the freedom, the right, and the responsibility to choose who we are to be and how to live our own lives. He argued that there was no essential human nature and no essential meaning to life, so we must make what we will of our subjective existence.

This freedom to find our own meaning for life requires a cynical mistrust of fixed social roles and parochial systems of belief. Those who accept responsibility for free choice in their individual existence can take pride in the conscious ways they define themselves. Unfortunately, some of his more naive and impatient young disciples took his assertion that life had no essential meaning too literally. To confirm symbolically what they thought they'd learned from existentialism, a few of these young French students committed suicide!

Sartre himself said, "My life and my philosophy are one in the same."[5] He lived out his philosophy publicly in radical social and political action and soon became an internationally influential personality, both as a novelist and playwright, as well as a philosopher and political activist.

He lived out his beliefs in his private life as well. His lover, Simone de Beauvoir, shared his standards for intimate personal relationship: "travel, polygamy, transparency."[6] In a large Parisian apartment, they led independent lives, often conversing with each other by phone. They lived together for fifty-one years without marrying, and every two years reconsidered and renewed, as agreed on, the option of whether or not to go on as partners.

The outcome of Sartre's transformation is best summed up in his own words: "Existentialism defines man by his actions. Man commits himself to his life, and thereby draws his image, beyond which there is nothing. We are alone without excuses. This is what I mean when I say that man is condemned to be free."[7]

Like all clearly defined individuals, Sartre polarized his audiences. Alternately admired for inspiring individual freedom and condemned for criticizing traditional values, his words called into question the beliefs of both his disciples and his detractors. He became a man who, in retrospect, could not think about his old ways of living without laughing at himself, and so to the end of his life, he was able to remain dedicated to going wherever his true self might lead him. He refused to accept the Legion of

Honor Medal, the Nobel Prize, and a chair at the College of France—all because he was unwilling to be defined by institutions, no matter how grand.

Sartre's successful transformations stand in sharp contrast to the failures of another believer in radical personal freedom, the Marquis de Sade. The central crises of this aristocratic libertine also involved the loss of liberty. He was imprisoned before he was thirty, first for debts and then for a scandalous affair in which he held four prostitutes against their will and subjected them to abuse. He was involved in a series of escapes and then in orgiastic incidents that resulted in further imprisonment. All in all, Sade spent more than twenty-eight of the last forty years of his life locked up.

He, too, tried to turn the crisis of imprisonment into an opportunity for personal growth. Although Sade attempted to transform his lechery into a philosophical outlook, he became little more than a pathological pornographer.

While in prison, he began to read voraciously—both the philosophical classics and the literary works of his time—and to write prolifically—novels, plays, and essays. In the end, Sade developed a violently antireligious and passionately irreverent philosophy of his own. He "had in mind to annotate every possible act or combination of acts of vice and every conceivable outrage."[8] His books were not intended as sex manuals that would shock his readers, but rather as philosophical works that would horrify, fascinate, and enlighten them, all at the same time.

Sade contended that human behavior is determined by nature rather than by any externally imposed system. In his "individual determination of morality,"[9] he insisted that "there is no evil from which some good does not result."[10]

He lived as he wrote, committing repeated scandalous acts of lechery during the brief times of escape from prison. After his release, he was appointed a judge by the French Revolutionary government. On the bench, he refused to sentence members of the opposition to death because "while one might commit crimes for the sake of pleasure," one must not "murder in the name of justice."[11]

Sartre's mistress, Simone de Beauvoir, later wrote an essay titled "Must We Burn Sade?"[12] insisting that Sade's aberrations were of less interest in themselves than in the ethical significance of his assuming responsibility for them. She believed that the primary value of his irreverent hedonism was its ability to unsettle us into reexamining all we've been taught in order to free our minds of restriction. In other words, *what goes on within our imagination is nobody's business but our own!*

By the time a woman I will call Melissa came to see me about her "self-destructive love relationship," my work with her had been informed by these writings. Melissa had spent much of her unhappy adult life attached to abusive men, most of whom she had married. Each time she had hoped that being part of a couple would make her feel good about herself, and allow her to "live happily ever after."

An earlier experience in psychotherapy had freed Melissa from the emotional battering of her third marriage. When she came to see me, she was in love with a homosexual man who had AIDS. As she put it, "I married one domineering, insensitive, macho bastard after another. Once I was able to escape from their abuse, I decided it was too dangerous to ever love again. Then what do I do, but fall for a faggot with AIDS! We'll never make love. He'll die; and I'll grow old alone. I guess I'm a real sicko."

During our first session we agreed to work together, but when I told Melissa that we'd have to meet at least twice a week, she insisted that other time commitments wouldn't allow her to come more than once a week. She interpreted my stipulation about how often we'd need to meet as implying that she was "so messed up emotionally" that I couldn't help her unless I saw her frequently. I explained that my requirement had less to do with the severity of *her* problems than with *my own* need to feel free to offer her the sort of help I wanted to provide.

Melissa pleaded with me to "compromise," but I stood fast. I offered her the names of other therapists who might agree to see her less frequently, but she refused my referrals and insisted that I was the only therapist she wanted to see.

Melissa left understanding that when she was ready to meet twice a week, she could call for another appointment. A few days later, I received a note telling me that although my behavior had been "unprofessional," unfortunately, once again she felt drawn to yet another abusive, unresponsive "hard-ass." She promised to call me when her time was freed up by fulfillment of her current commitments.

A couple of months later, we began meeting twice a week. Although Melissa prided herself on being "a special sort of person" whose brassy, "freely flamboyant" behavior was "outrageous," I saw her nonconformity as a superficial attempt to shock other people with what she called her "gutter-mouth" speech, to dazzle them with her "glitzy" appearance, and to spook them with her "voodoo" belief in the occult.

During her time in therapy with me, Melissa reported

a series of dreams of which this one is typical: "I found myself in the sort of cottage I'd always dreamed of someday having when I was young, but now that I'd gotten it, everything was all wrong! The view from the windows was obscured by lacy curtains that were too billowy, and blocked by a white picket fence that was too tall. I knew that the surrounding landscape was gorgeous but I couldn't see any of it from where I stood. I turned away so that at least I could enjoy the inside of my house, but everything there was screwed up, too. All I can remember about the living room is that somehow I'd hung all of the pictures upside down."

She understood her dream to mean that her mother had been right when she said that even if Melissa got everything she wanted, her daughter would never be happy because she always managed to mess things up. Instead, I suggested that the problems with her dream house indicated she had a needlessly restricted outlook, symbolized by the overly decorated windows. Her view of herself and her life was obstructed by her false sense of flamboyance as freedom and cluttered with her exaggerated sense of what is acceptable. I invited her to imagine that these pretensions kept her from enjoying the beautiful landscape that lay right before her eyes.

Melissa viewed her "falling for a faggot" as an indication that she was still "screwed up," but I found her descriptions of that relationship much more loving than her experiences with all the other eligible men she'd known. When I told her, "It sounds as though you've never before cared as deeply or been treated so tenderly," her usual cynical tone gave way to a softer, sweeter voice than I'd ever heard from her.

She began to cry in spite of herself, all the while protesting that "if there's no sex, it's got to be sick." When I suggested that she couldn't believe that any man could possibly love her unless he wanted to go to bed with her, she sobbed more deeply. Melissa tried to deny the poignancy of all she felt by pulling herself together, resuming her street-smart veneer and insisting, "Yeah, yeah, but what kind of a dumb bitch gets hooked on a guy who she knows is about to croak?"

I answered softly, "A woman who, for the first time in her life, has courage enough to put the love she feels ahead of the loss she fears." That day Melissa cried openly, without constraint, dealing with the depth of her heartfelt feelings for as long as she could, and later returning to grieve them again and again.

Gradually, she began to see that what was most important wasn't whether or not the relationship made sense, but simply that she felt free to love again. What mattered most was that Melissa was following her heart in a way that was emotionally meaningful for her at this particular time of her life.

If all she'd wanted was to settle the crisis this relationship had created, she would have left therapy at that point. Instead, she stayed on, excited about whatever other newfound freedoms this unexpected understanding might prefigure.

We returned to interpreting her dream several sessions later when Melissa was discussing her career crisis. After her divorce, she had entered graduate school to become a social worker. She described it as "a lark," saying, "What's an unmarried girl to do for a living? I know I'm sitting on a fortune, but I hate men too much to be a hooker." I suggested that the reasons she'd decided not to become a prostitute were because she didn't hate men enough and because she wasn't sufficiently shallow to turn tricks for a living.

Additionally, I pointed out that in any case, social work wasn't her only alternative and that she was unlikely to have chosen that path at random. Begrudgingly, Melissa admitted that even though she usually thought of herself as "totally self-indulgent," she felt a deep longing to relieve other people's suffering and to make something worthwhile out of what she saw as her own squandered life.

She wanted to be a psychotherapist, but believed that once I learned that she used tarot readings[13] and other "voodoo" in her practice, I would see to it that she got her walking papers. It was difficult for Melissa to believe that I could take such nontraditional efforts seriously.

I view the folk art we call psychotherapy as no more than a contemporary Western form of the age-old, universal, soul-making attempt of one human being to help another through life's unavoidable common crises of disappointment and loss. Whatever works to allow both the therapist and the patient to discover ways to become more aware of their options and of responsibility for their decisions seems all right to me.

The assumption that early childhood experiences are the basis of needless adult suffering works well for the psychoanalysts who see therapy as the patient telling his or her story to find out how it began. But in my mind, neurosis and the Oedipus complex are no more than psychoanalytic metaphors.

Many therapists use other imagery with equal effectiveness. Some patients have found peace in the present by exploring past lives and others have transformed their lives by being rebirthed. Melissa's voodoo might work as well for her and for those she wanted to help.

I returned to her dream, inviting Melissa to understand the pictures she'd hung upside down as imagery related to her fascination with Tarot readings. The archetypal images of the Tarot cards "transcend cultural and linguistic conventions."[14]

Many people use these cards for telling fortunes. I see them as reflecting the hidden unconscious recesses of ourselves that have been obscured to comply with conventional wisdom. The Hanged Man is a pivotal card in the pack, an image that symbolizes standing at the threshold of transformation. The figure hangs suspended upside down from a cross of living wood. Arms folded behind his back, forming a living cross with his unfettered leg, his head hangs down in a bright cloud of deep entrancement. He is in a position of reversal of mind, doing penance for how he has made his way in the world till then as he surrenders to the redemption of absorption in matters both spiritual and occult.

In the upright position, this card suggests the reversal of a person's way of life. During this prophetic pause, he or she suspends decisions while on the verge of yielding completely to consciousness of all that had previously been ignored. Reversed, the card implies false prophecy, arrogance, and resistances to spiritual influences. Its appearance indicates a crucial crossroads, at which the individual is in crisis—either headed for redemption or just hung up.

For a while, Melissa and I talked in Tarot imagery of

the pictures hung upside down in her dream. Once she experienced my acceptance of her idiosyncratic ways of working, she began to explore the worth of her personal peculiarities without worrying as much about their legitimacy.

At her request, I undertook some supervision of her work. Gradually, she became less and less concerned about her "freaky" deviance from the norms and, eventually, also felt comfortable about asserting her freedom to do therapy that was very different from the ways I worked.

Before the death of the male homosexual she loved, Melissa gradually transformed their relationship into her first reliable, mutually respectful friendship with a man. While he lived, she shifted her therapeutic activity to working with AIDS patients. After he died, she began serving as a counselor to the dying at a local hospice.

It turned out that Melissa's search for romantic love was not over. She began an exploration of Lesbian relationships that she expected to result in "a delayed coming out of the closet." Her fantasy of becoming "a diesel-dyke" was a short-term experiment. These explorations failed to turn her into a homosexual, but they did free her to have friendships with other women that were less emotionally constricted than any she'd ever had before.

It was then that Melissa was able to reclaim her desire for a heterosexual man with whom to share her life. This time her search was uncluttered by the traditional image of herself as a dependent woman who could only be made complete by marriage to a macho character who would take care of her.

Instead she wanted a sensitive, accepting man who

would treat her with respect without feeling threatened by her having a life of her own. She had rich friendships with both men and women and a career that was clearly of her own making. For the first time, she was able to envision love free of the clinging dependency that had previously left her so vulnerable to abuse.

Melissa had discovered that *the extent of her freedom to live a life that was truly her own depended on her ability to distinguish what she wanted from all that others expected of her.*

There's nothing wrong with choosing to go along with the crowd, so long as we do it with full awareness of all that our decision implies. To be true to ourselves, we need only be aware of our options, choose among them deliberately, and take responsibility for facing the consequences of our actions.

Freedom of the will doesn't demand that we defy conventional wisdom. It only requires that when we conform to arbitrarily set communal standards, we understand that we have chosen an alternative that we can as readily decline. It feels good to know that we can do what's expected, but sometimes it feels better when we don't. As a young jazz pianist once said, "I'd like to be able to play like Art Tatum, and then not."

No matter how hard we try, we cannot *will* either our freedom or the fulfillment of our goals. We cannot accomplish personal and spiritual growth simply by deciding to change our lives. Instead we must lose ourselves to experiencing the moment, and leave our development to the higher power that is hidden within ourselves.

For example, a tale is told of a wise man who went off on a religious retreat. He had decided to try to attain spiritual growth by enduring an ordeal of fasting, but just in case he got too hungry during his week in seclusion, he took along several loaves of bread and a pitcher of water. When he was ready to go home at the end of the week, he lifted his sack, felt how heavy it was, and, opening it, found to his great surprise that all the loaves were still in it. It was then he realized that fasting by forgetting hunger during devotion to prayer feels fine.[15]

7

To Be Creative, We Have to Follow Our Feelings

After the leader of a religious community died, he was replaced by his son. When members of the congregation complained that the young man's ways were different from his father's, the son replied, "I am doing just as my father did. He did not imitate and neither do I."[1]

If we want our efforts to be original and creative, we must be willing to lose interest in wondering what other people think of the ways we work. We have to be careful about getting caught between concentration on our own inner vision and the distraction of other people watching what we're doing. Two well-known American artists grappled with this kind of crisis, each in her own way. Georgia O'Keeffe[2] was a painter and Diane Arbus[3] was a photographer. Because they were both women working in fields traditionally dominated by men, the critical acclaim their work merited was awarded begrudgingly.

O'Keeffe was raised by a farm family who paid little attention to her. She died in her nineties after having lived a professionally prolific and personally fulfilling life. Arbus was a culturally advantaged child of a wealthy New York family. She committed suicide in her fifties by slitting her wrists.

O'Keeffe's early interest in painting was only accepted by her family because they thought that she might "become an accomplished young lady or even an art teacher."[4] No one except Georgia herself took seriously the idea that she might someday actually become an artist. She was always an independent, self-directed loner who resisted interference by others and kept her own counsel. As a young feminist, she believed that any entanglement would restrict her artistic freedom, and she shied away from romance to conserve her energy for her painting.

Eventually, O'Keeffe's studied aloofness was challenged by her encounter with Alfred Stieglitz. This insistently aggressive, considerably older man was a successful New York photographer who ran an internationally influential gallery that promoted the work of young artists.

Because O'Keeffe was such a private person, she "recoiled at the idea of strangers viewing her paintings,"[5] but Stieglitz believed in her talent, overrode her protests, and showed her work to the world. He fell in love with her as a woman and celebrated her as an artist.

O'Keeffe yielded to him on both fronts—going public as an artist and surrendering to his demands for domesticity. She lived with Stieglitz for many years and then reluctantly agreed to marry him. Although she wanted to live in the desert of the Southwest that inspired her painting, she agreed to stay in New York City, where he wanted to live.

She was gradually accepted as an important "woman artist," and her pictures were often interpreted as expressing a peculiarly female, erotic vision of life. O'Keeffe's crisis amounted to getting caught in a crunch when both her husband and the art world gave precedence to her identity as a woman over her own priority of seeing herself as an artist.

She met the career crisis by stalwartly asserting that her original way of seeing things reflected her free, creative vision as an artist, rather than a gender-bound outlook as a female. She affirmed her individuality by stating, "The men like to put me down by seeing me as the best *woman* painter. I think I'm one of the best painters."[6]

She found maintaining her independence from Stieglitz more difficult. Her aging, possessive husband felt hurt when she wanted to go off to New Mexico to paint. O'Keeffe began to suffer from severe headaches and hypersensitivity to noise. As her distress intensified, she became terrified of going out onto the crowded city streets and began to fear that she was losing her mind. After being hospitalized for several weeks, she decided to defy Stieglitz's wishes by returning to the Southwest to be "fully individuated and alone, upon a mesa."[7]

To survive as an artist, she continued this pattern of "setting out from the East each Spring with tubes of paint and rolls of canvas and returning in the Autumn with her back seat full of paintings for Stieglitz to show to the world."[8] He settled for accepting six months a year with her, rather than twelve months with any other woman in the world.

After her husband died, O'Keeffe spent most of the rest of her life living alone in the desert where she could paint without being distracted by domestic demands or public pressures. She lived her life as a lone, strong woman; an independent, private person; and a creative, prolific painter—adamantly self-assured in her reticence about her work and brazenly undisguised in her defiance of conventional social demands.

Both attitudes are clearly expressed in her impatient reactions to intrusive strangers. One asked why she didn't sign her work and O'Keeffe replied, "Why don't you sign your face?"[9] Another arrived unannounced at the gate of her secluded mountain home and asked to see Georgia O'Keeffe. " 'Front side!' she declared, then turned and announced, 'Back side!' then turned again and said, 'Goodbye!' and slammed the gate."[10]

She was not so much a misanthropic recluse as she was simply someone who was very particular about how she ran her life. I remember having seen a documentary,[11] filmed by Perry Miller Adato when O'Keeffe was in her eighties. When a partial loss of vision interrupted her painting, she allowed a young potter to move in with her. O'Keeffe was happy to have this moustached, pony-tailed young man teach her how to make hand-rolled pottery. Her energy was sufficiently restored that gradually she began to paint again.

Faced with the crisis our culture often imposes on ambitious women, O'Keeffe put painting first and set domestic life second. She ignored what society expected of her, and setting her sights through the eyes of her soul, went her own way, lived a long and happy life, and brought the beauty of her personal vision to the world.

This woman's liberation had a glorious outcome, but as

the next woman's experiences show, true stories don't always have happy endings. Diane Arbus faced a comparable crisis, made a similar decision, and ended up a casualty of her attempts to claim her own place in the world. Although her unsettling, professional portraits of freaks and eccentrics "drastically altered our sense of what is permissible in photography,"[12] her personal alienation and disillusionment became so overwhelming that she ended up killing herself.

She, too, had been a very private, excruciatingly shy child, but unlike O'Keeffe, Arbus was raised by demanding parents who imposed their own self-absorbed social reality on their secretly imaginative, highly gifted child. They used her as a compliant ornament for their own uncertain egos and their abusive intrusion proved more deadly than the benign neglect that O'Keeffe had suffered as a child. Arbus soon became unsure of who or what she was, and of the boundaries between herself and others.

She identified with Lewis Carroll's Alice, who changed from big to small in a kaleidoscopic world of shifting realities and illogical, mercurial rules. She stared for hours at her own reflection in the bathroom mirror, asking herself, "Am I really big? Am I really small? Am I in any way imperfect? Am I just right?"[13]

When she was thirteen, Arbus attempted to alleviate the anxieties caused by her childhood by attaching herself adoringly to a sophisticated, "tender but dominating"[14] man whom she referred to as her guru. They looked so much alike, they might have been twins.

Eventually she married Allan Arbus and tried hard to be his perfect housewife/mother. He decided that they would also work together as photographers, doing advertising layouts first for Diane's father's department store and later for slick high-fashion magazines.

The pressure of her constricted personal and professional life turned into a crisis that left Arbus deeply depressed. Although she was terrified of being alone, she began to understand that her life would count for little unless she lived it on her own terms.

Arbus attempted to break loose by exploring a series of unconventional sexual experiments. She admitted that her hunger for unusual experiences was so extreme that she even envied a woman friend who had been raped. "Sex was the quickest, most primitive way to begin connecting with another human being, and the raunchier and grosser the person or environment, the more intense her experience, and the more it enlarged her life."[15] Eventually, her erotic escapades resulted in the breakup of her marriage.

Once she was free of her devotion to her perfectionistic, domineering partner in photography, Arbus began to experience the emergence of her own distinctive artistic vision. She wanted to photograph whatever she viewed as grotesque and forbidden—the external images of all that was hidden within her secret self.

Arbus took pictures of leathery, retired midgets; giants; tattooed people; odd pairs of twins; and overweight nudists as well as "the androgynous, the crippled, the dead, and the dying."[16] She was both fascinated and repulsed by her subjects. To do her work, she had to find the courage to face her own sense of being a freak.

Getting permission to photograph at nudist camps required that she be naked, too. As she put it, "I'm not vicarious, I'm involved."[17] This was true of her personal life as well. The more successful she became at working with her camera, the more aggressively and eccentrically she pursued her erotic experimentation until the two activities intertwined. In her words, "Taking a portrait is like seducing someone." [18] Although she was excited by danger, Arbus succumbed more and more frequently to bouts of helplessness and hopelessness.

When not denounced as a horror show, her controversial work was acclaimed by many critics for its singular impact on a field previously dominated by men. As Norman Mailer put it, "Giving a camera to Diane Arbus is like giving a hand grenade to a baby." [19] Eventually she turned over one rock too many and out crawled some aspect of herself that seemed so awful to her that she killed herself.

When my client is an artist, I sometimes find the biographical images of O'Keeffe and Arbus useful extremes in staking out the intertwining of personality and career. An exceedingly intellectualized, overcontrolled young artist whom I will call Jean came to see me because he felt paralyzed about going on with his painting. He'd already undergone some psychotherapy in another city a few years earlier. He described the therapist fondly as having relieved him of "episodes of deep depression resulting from conflicts about expressing anger left over from childhood."

Jean wondered whether the current symptom he called "artist's block" was yet another reaction to the poor parenting he'd suffered in childhood. He described his mother as so intrusive that he'd yearned to tell her to back off. Jean complained that even though his father kept emotionally distant, he often undermined his son's self-confidence.

Jean described his most recent problems in this way: "I've been an art student for years, but I've never been able to master a style I could claim as my own. Whenever I sketch or paint a still-life or a portrait, it always ends up looking like someone else's work. I gave up on attempting representational pictures to see what I could accomplish with cubism, surrealism, and abstract expressionism. Now, I can produce an adequate piece of craftsmanship, but all my canvasses look like examples of a particular period, and never like the work of the artist I believe I can some-day be."

Jean went on to describe how, in desperation, he'd given up trying to learn to paint, began studying art his-tory, and lately had turned to exploring "the philosophical subtext of art." He had come to understand the artist's role in society, the place of art as an event in the experi-ence of the audience, and the interconnectedness of art and life. "But," he complained, "knowing all of that, I can't pick up a brush without feeling intimidated by imag-ining the impossibility of improving on the aesthetic per-fection of a blank canvas."

I responded sympathetically by saying, "You long to let your own image emerge, but your productions always look like someone else's work, painted in another time and place." Jean began to speak excitedly about having always felt that he couldn't tell who he really was and of his hope that painting would someday allow his true self to emerge. When he spoke of this longing for emergence, Jean appeared to get very tense and shifted to talking about having other troubles besides being "a failed painter." He described his disappointing attempts to establish a long-term relationship with a woman.

I said, "When you talk about exposing your real self, you become anxious and shift to describing your failed relationships with women instead. You intend to change the subject, but the two issues intertwine." Jean flushed and squirmed uncomfortably, opened and closed his mouth several times as if he were about to speak, and then changed his mind, cleared his throat, and began to gasp for air.

I said softly, "You struggle with trying to decide whether or not to tell me something unspeakable about yourself. It sticks in your throat. You can't quite spit it out, but you can't swallow it either. When you're ready, you'll tell me what you want me to know."

It took several sessions for Jean to reveal the secret he'd kept hidden throughout his earlier therapy—his certainty that he was a homosexual. He also described some sketches and paintings that he hadn't been able to tell me about before—productions he called "gay pornography."

A few sessions later Jean recounted this transformation dream: "I dreamed that there were strange sounds coming from behind a closed closet door and that there was a silhouette of a woman standing still and silent, as if waiting for something to happen. She hadn't done anything wrong, but I screamed at her to go away. The woman didn't move and the sounds from the closet turned out to be a child saying, 'Dada.' I tried to ignore both of them— as if I had more important things on my mind."

He offered a textbook interpretation of the dream as yet another demonstration of how his unhappy childhood had resulted in his inability to relate to a woman or to parent a child of his own. I suggested that Jean make overtures to the dream figure with the same humility he might muster in approaching his muse—as if she might have something to teach him that he didn't already know.

I pointed out that the woman he had dismissed in his dream could be viewed as his own feminine aspect—not his homosexuality, but his creative spirit. Using guided imagery, I invited Jean to imagine that instead of driving off the dark woman in his dream, he ask her what she was waiting for. When he tried this, he was astonished to discover that, instead of intruding as his mother would have done, the dark lady said that she was ready to share with him whatever secrets of hers that might be of help. It was not only Jean's homosexuality that he needed to bring out of the closet, but the higher power within him as well.

I went on to reinterpret the image of the baby as an image of yet another part of himself—his future growth, crying out to be acknowledged and taken care of. When I suggested that its outcry of "dada" could also be seen as a veiled reference to the rebellious artists' movement dadaism, Jean immediately acknowledged his fascination with that elusive, contradictory, antiartistic movement that had sired surrealism.

Dada's wholehearted, unremitting assault on the norms imposed by any oppressive cultural system was an outcry for creative freedom. "The enduring message of dada was, 'Anything goes!'."[20] Some unconventional, original artists accidentally discovered the word *dada* in a Swiss dictionary. It is a brief, suggestive, French word for a wooden horse; a senseless, comic bit of baby prattle; ideally suited to their wish to spoof serious people, particularly when the dadaists used the term to signify nothing in particular.

The movement protested against conventional and official art by putting forth absurd parodies—exhibiting a urinal titled *The Fountain* and having an artist sign a bottle-drying rack to confer on it the status of a sculpture. With irony and irreverence, both parodies were intended to demonstrate that every form of expression is potentially artistic. Dada was "against past art, not because it was art but because it was past."[21]

The antic iconoclasm of dada toppled conventional authority's claims on the creativity of the artists, insisting that "true dadaists are against dada and that everyone is a leader of the dada movement."[22] With much laughter, Jean and I talked at length of the need for perpetual artistic revolution and of dada's irony of indifference.

Jean went on to come out of the closet to become a supporter of gay pride. Once he accepted his homosexuality as a life worth living, his "gay pornographic cartooning" gave way to softer sketches of men treating one another tenderly—men who loved one another.

This was just the beginning of his transformation. Once he'd learned to honor his pecularities, Jean's artistic efforts broadened to a wide range of wonderful paintings *in a style all his own*. He'd found a creative form of expression that was neither homosexual nor heterosexual—a personal vision that seemed simply human.

If we want to be creative, we must learn to care less about how we will look in the eyes of others than what we feel about what we are doing. For the audience, an artistic production is only a public event; for the artist, it is a personal experience. But *it is not the outcome but our input that counts*. The rewards of our work come from the individual efforts we put into them. Public acceptance is simply a fringe benefit.

A tale is told of a teacher and his disciples watching a

tightrope walker who was so absorbed in what he was doing that they asked their teacher what it was that riveted the aerialist's gaze to this seemingly foolish performance. The teacher answered, "I cannot say why this man is risking his life. I only know that while he is up there, he is not thinking of the gold coins he is earning by walking the rope—for if he did, he would fall."[23]

8

Humility Helps Us Find Our Way

❧ Once there was a holy man whose apprentice served him diligently. The only reason that the master kept him on was because of the disciple's dedication. Otherwise he found the fellow rather stupid.

One day, a rumor spread throughout the region that the acolyte had walked on water, fording the river as easily as if he were crossing the street. The master questioned him about this miraculous accomplishment, "Is it possible that what people are saying about you is true? Can you really cross the river walking on the water?"

"What could be more natural?" answered the apprentice. "It is thanks to you, O Blessed One, that I walked on water. At every step, I repeated your saintly name and that is what held me up."

The holy man thought to himself, "If the lowly disciple can walk on water, what can the master not do? If it is in my name that the miracle takes place, I must possess power I did not suspect and holiness of which I have been unaware. After all, I have never tried to ford the river as if I was crossing the street."

The master ran to the riverbank. Without hesitation, he set his foot on the water, and with unshakable faith he chanted, "Me, me, me." And he sank.[1]

This story serves as a warning. When we commit our lives to a cause, we must take care not to mistake believing in our own inflated egos for faith in altruistic goals. Malcolm X[2] and Abbie Hoffman,[3] both magnetic personalities, found themselves at crossroads that would allow them to become charismatic leaders.

One chose a religious path that catapulted him into a position as a leader in the cause of restoring the self-esteem of his oppressed people. He was willing to risk his life to inspire desperately needed social changes. The other set out to liberate a generation of restless youths and made a major contribution to a passing countercultural phase, now nostalgically known as the 1960s generation. He became a personality cult figure who ended up as a fugitive fleeing imprisonment by going underground, and dying of an intentional overdose of drugs.

It was while he was still in prison that Malcolm's identity was transformed from convicted con man to Black Muslim convert. He became enthralled by the teachings of Elijah Muhammad, the elder of the Lost-Found Nation of Islam, whose interpretation of the Koran reflected the situation of oppressed American blacks. These teachings inspired Malcolm's realization that he had a viable alternative to his critical dilemma—whether to choose being a criminal or living like a slave.

Elijah Muhammad taught that the white man was a blue-eyed devil who was losing his power to oppress and exploit dark-skinned people. He instructed his followers that Allah wanted them to restore the glorious, black African civilizations that existed before their people were enslaved.

In keeping with these teachings, Malcolm X condemned whites publicly for what blacks, up till then, had only accused them of privately. When he was a boy, his own father had been killed by white vigilantes. As a man, he stood before white audiences and told them, "Your father isn't here to pay his debts. My father isn't here to collect. But I'm here to collect, and you're here to pay."[4]

In the civil rights movement, Martin Luther King, Jr., and Malcolm X "arrived at the crossroad from opposite directions, the one out of the seminary and the other the penitentiary. They stood at opposite poles in the national consciousness—Christian and Muslim, idealist and cynic, pacifist and warrior, color-blind and color-conscious."[5] Dr. King inspired integration through nonviolence, while Malcolm X fired up his followers on separatism and the power of actively fighting back against whites. Although they were never formally allied, together they made an inspiring black leadership team.

Unlike Malcolm X, Abbie Hoffman grew up in a family that had not been beaten down by an oppressive society. Although he was expelled from high school for assaulting a teacher who tore up his paper affirming atheism, he graduated elsewhere, completed college, and went on to complete a master's degree in psychology. For three years, he worked as a psychologist at a state mental hospital, but left, tired of trying to help one person at a time and convinced that the problems to be solved didn't lie in the minds of the patients, but in the society that had confused them.

He campaigned in support of the Committee for a Sane Nuclear Policy and next as an American Civil Liberties Union organizer against the House Un-American Activities Committee (HUAC). For a while, he worked as a pharmaceutical salesman whose work on the road allowed him to get paid for taking off to participate in the Southern civil rights movement. This delighted him because, "Not only was I ripping off the company in the traditional way, but a right-wing corporation was unwittingly underwriting a civil rights organizer."[6]

He attributes the crisis that shaped the rest of his life to witnessing "two generation-shaking events" that happened within a week in May 1960: a demonstration against capital punishment,[7] in which he participated, and the "Bloody Friday" protest against HUAC.[8] The brutal beating of the protesters by the police made Abbie's savage indignation toward authority the central pivot of the rest of his life.

Together with Jerry Rubin, he went on to organize the Yippies (Youth International Party), an irreverent and zany countercultural movement that attempted to change the course of history by putting flowers into the rifle barrels of the troops called out to keep them from "levitating" the Pentagon; hurling dollar bills from the gallery of the New York Stock Exchange, creating pandemonium among the brokers below; and holding a counterconvention[9] that ended in a police riot in the streets.

Abbie paid his dues. He was harassed, beaten, arrested, and jailed for his leadership of the anti-Vietnam War movement. Believing that LSD was a way of seeing beyond the destructive propaganda of the establishment, he did a lot of drugs. Eventually, he was arrested, first for possession and later for the sale of cocaine. While on the run as a fugitive with a changed identity, he continued to organize efforts to protect the environment. But when he was fifty-three he killed himself perhaps because his "revolution for the hell of it" had failed.

Malcolm X had committed his life to the cause of remedying the destructive effects of racial prejudice by enabling a despairing minority to reclaim responsibility for their future. His leadership helped transform their self-hatred into group pride, and their crime-ridden ghettos into self-directed communities of law-abiding Black Muslims who abstained from alcohol, drugs, and stealing.

Abbie Hoffman also committed his life to a cause but he confused who he was with what he believed in. The statement in his autobiography that most clearly expresses this contamination of principle by ego is, "There is absolutely no greater high than challenging the power structure as a nobody, giving it your all, and winning."[10]

I once treated a man I will call Carlos, who was also dedicated to improving the lot of oppressed people. Although Carlos was never destructive, his efforts were occasionally misguided. He had grown up as the youngest child in a large family of overachieving siblings and had hungered all his life for a place of importance in the world.

My patient had achieved some success as a student, and then as a teacher of political science. Although he loved his wife and children, Carlos continued to feel restless and vaguely dissatisfied with himself.

Previous therapy had enhanced his self-esteem and allowed him to become sufficiently self-assertive to be a political activist. Eventually, he'd attained recognition and respect in the New Left, both as a participant in the Freedom Summer civil rights marches and as an organizer in the Vietnam peace movement.

By the time he came to see me, Carlos felt exhilarated about his political activities, but despondent because his marriage was coming apart. His career left him so little time and energy to spend at home that his family felt neglected. Recently, his wife had learned about his one-night stands with movement groupies and had threatened to leave him.

Early in our work together, Carlos dreamed that he was walking down an unpaved country road. In the distance, he could hear hoofbeats and see the dust raised by a rag-tag peasant army singing a simple, stirring song. He thought to himself, "Here come my followers."

Carlos stopped and stood at the side of the road waiting for the column to approach. He had expected them to halt when they reached him and couldn't comprehend why they went on without stopping to acknowledge him as their leader. He was astonished when he saw that the column was headed by a corpse tied to the lead horse.

Just after the troops had passed, the last rider turned and motioned to Carlos to join them. When the dream ended, he was still standing by the side of the road, trying to decide what to do.

Carlos interpreted the dream as yet another expression of his lifelong feeling that as the youngest child in his family he would always come last. I suggested that instead, he allow himself to imagine that this dream had less to say about his past than about his present, and perhaps about his future as well.

I asked Carlos if he knew the legend of El Cid. Although the name was familiar, he couldn't remember the story. I told him the tale of the medieval Spanish leader who had so thoroughly confused his own inflated ego with the cause for which he fought that he believed his people could not possibly prevail unless he himself led them.

After a series of battles, El Cid was wounded. That night, as he lay dying, he ordered his aides to tie his dead body to his horse the next morning. His last words were, "The people will not be able to go on without seeing that I still lead them. I am their heart."

Carlos could acknowledge El Cid's arrogance, but not his own. He insisted that people cannot overcome oppression unless they see their cause personified in a charismatic leader. I agreed that might be the case at times, but I went on to suggest that it's one thing for the followers to see their leader as God—it's another for the leader to make the same mistake.

At first, Carlos found it difficult to relinquish his inflated sense of how much he meant to the movement, but as his self-importance diminished, he was once again able to enjoy his commitment to a cause more significant than his idealized image of himself. He also began to understand that the groupies he had used so impersonally had taken advantage of him in the process he'd almost lost the family that was the heart of his personal life. As if for the first time, Carlos realized that if he couldn't treat lovingly the particular people who meant the most to him his devotion to humankind meant little.

When we discover that our lives feel empty of meaning, one way we can resolve this crisis is by devoting ourselves to a worthwhile movement that will benefit the community. A spiritual leader who believed that it was his mission to reform the community once said that, in his youth, he was so fired with the love of God he thought he would convert the whole world. After a short time, he decided that it would be quite an accomplishment if he could just convert the people who lived in his village. Even in this more modest mission, he did not succeed.

When he realized that he was still being too ambitious, he concentrated on the people in his own household, but he could not convert them either. In the end, it dawned on this self-appointed savior that his main ministry had to be to work on himself. If he couldn't convert anyone else, at least he might offer his own true service to God. Shortly before his death, he had to admit that he had not fully accomplished even that.[11]

9

Opening Our Hearts to Others

A holy man who was leaving on a trip to a spiritual retreat invited some of his followers to share his carriage. For fear that they would crowd him, they were reluctant to accept his invitation. When he learned of their hesitance, he offered them the reassurance that "If we allow ourselves to love each other more, then there will be room for everyone."[1]

Spiritual seeking starts out with oneself, but it does not end with oneself. We must learn to understand ourselves fully without remaining preoccupied *only* with ourselves.

During the first half of his life, Thomas Merton[2] was a heavy drinker, an avid party goer, and a lover of many women. In the second half of his life, he was a Trappist monk who was concerned with social issues and who helped bring Buddhism to the West.

Bhagwan Shree Rajneesh[3] was a charismatic Oriental

swami. He desecrated the power of his religious leadership by organizing frequent sexual orgies, fleeing his followers of money, and ending up owning more Rolls Royces than anyone else in the world. Both men transformed their lives at points of spiritual crises, but one opened the souls he touched to an enlightened meeting of sacred and worldly issues, while the other exploited his followers financially and emotionally.

Thomas Merton's transformation did not occur until well into his adult life, but when he attained his spiritual commitment, from that time on he saw it as a never-ending search because "between seeking and finding lies the tension of human life."[4]

Merton's party going was diverting, but left him feeling empty and restless. His other major interest was writing, but after he read Dante[5] he realized that because he had not yet been recognized as a writer his injured pride had made him impervious to accepting all that God was offering him. As he put it, "The mere realization of one's own unhappiness is not salvation: it may be the occasion of salvation, or it may be the door to a deeper pit in the Hell"[6] —a pit from which he was already trying to escape. Vanity had made a mess of Merton's life and he knew it. Unless he cleaned it up, he would never find a way out of his misery. It was then that he fell in love with a woman who treated him as carelessly as he had treated women who had loved him. For the first time in his adult life, Merton felt a fear from which his usual entertainments could not distract him.

Paradoxically, it was in this new crisis that he turned toward Christ for love. All at once, he became aware that he'd been starving in the midst of plenty. His newfound hunger was so intense that he read voraciously about both Christian and Oriental mysticism.

During this immersion in mysticism, he began to "retreat from the fight for money and fame and from the active and worldly life of conflict and competition",[7] to move toward the spiritual life of peace and detachment. He was drawn toward the Catholic church but was beset by one decision and revision after another—first he believed that all he needed was to become a convert, next he wanted to study for the priesthood, then he chose to enter a monastery of the Franciscan order, and eventually claimed his vocation as a Trappist monk.

Merton saw the life of a Trappist monk as his best chance for saving himself from his own enormous ego. Ironically, once he had willingly divested himself of his personal identity as a writer, his Trappist superiors instructed him that writing was to be his vocation. He was to live the cloistered life while informing the community in the service of a higher power.

God had taken Merton to the edge by asking him to renounce his excessive social life and to undertake a vow of silence. Once the young monk had surrendered, giving up who he thought he was, he was told to return to the place he'd started from—to return home transformed by honoring his own peculiarities in a new way.

The spiritual journey is never ending. Merton closes his autobiography with the words "SIT FINIS LIBRI, NON FINIS QUAERENDI"[8] (Let this be the end of the book, not of the searching).

The transformation of Bhagwan Shree Rajneesh is an altogether different story. For years, he had seen communism as his path toward helping others. When that no longer seemed to satisfy his search for the meaning of his life, he immersed himself in spiritual studies and renounced his concern with the economic well-being of the world. His solitary pursuit of the spiritual life arose out of an emotional crisis characterized by a refusal to eat, the development of mysterious psychosomatic symptoms, and a suicide attempt. However, once he felt he had attained enlightenment, he declared that there is only one Enlightened Master in the world at any one time and that he was the one.[9]

He opened an Esalen-type center in India and became known as "the sex guru." Eventually he moved both his followers and his fame to America. Although he had started out as a celibate, he ended up a lecher. He began as a self-styled saint who wanted to save souls and became a demon who encouraged drug dealing and prostitution.

In the midst of her own spiritual crisis, a poet I will call Anne came to see me. She'd undergone therapy before—a partially successful healing she hoped had transformed her from an incest victim to "an incest survivor."

The primary damage suffered by victims of incest is the sense of betrayal children feel when they have been sexually molested by the parents they loved and depended on to take care of them. For a long while, Anne's attempts to cope with that damage had amounted to little more than wandering bewildered through a world filled with menace while engaging in any addiction that numbed her pain.

Uncertain about who she was and knowing for sure only how much she hurt, Anne spent many years in the stupor of drugs, alcohol, and physically dangerous, impersonally degrading discipline and bondage with strangers who were willing to use her sexually—just as she used them.

It wasn't much of a life, but it provided the perverse

illusion of control she needed to quiet the panicky feelings of helplessness and desperation that otherwise plagued her. Her previous therapy had brought her addictive acting out to an end. Once it was over, she had turned to religion, hoping to attain the inner peace she'd always longed for.

Anne came to see me, complaining that she was not spiritually pure enough to forgive her father. It hadn't yet occurred to her that instead she might need to forgive herself. Although she laughed with relief when I told her that I hadn't ever had a pure motive in my life, the belief that she could accept herself *as is* still eluded her.

She hoped that spirituality would add something to her personality. I believed that soulfulness would allow her to find that nothing about being human was alien to her and that everything about her might be worth something.

Anne recounted a transformation dream in which she was standing at the edge of a sweet, clear pool of water. She wanted to immerse herself so that God would redeem her, but every time she stepped into the pool, she stirred up the ooze at the bottom, muddied the waters, and jumped back out in horror.

Anne interpreted this dream as meaning that she was still so contaminated that she dirtied everything she touched. I suggested that she allow herself to imagine getting back into the pool, feeling whatever she must about sullying the waters, try to sit patiently, and see what happened next. To her relief, she found that the ooze eventually settled back to the bottom of the pool. As the debris floated downward, it created intriguingly intricate patterns in the waters that till then had been vacuously clear.

I told Anne about a mystic called Saint Teresa of Avila.

At a time when the cruelly watchful eye of the Spanish Inquisition was attempting to seek and destroy any signs of spontaneity among Christians, this sixteenth-century nun successfully instituted spiritually liberating reforms. At the risk of being executed for heresy, she courageously replaced the way of fear with the way of love by transforming worship from the traditional practice of impersonal, dogmatic ritual to the personally intimate prayer of an inner dialogue with God. In that place where she met the higher power within herself, Teresa discovered the rapture of "an honest awareness of how much all loves have in common."[10]

I told Anne my favorite story about Saint Teresa. It is a tale that demonstrates the pitiless honesty of her soulful insistence on laughing at herself without bitterness, while still stubbornly retaining her personal identity as a part of her religious life.

Early every morning, Teresa left the convent to ride her mule through the woods. When she was crossing a stream at the dawning of a particularly cold winter day, the mule bucked, tossing the robust nun into the icy stream. Sitting on her cold, wet backside, Teresa looked up at the Heavens and in a curious combination of irritation and amusement, said, "Dear Lord, if this is the way You treat Your friends, it's no wonder You have so few."

First Anne laughed, and then she cried. Eventually, she began to understand that she was asking more purity of herself than was humanly possible to attain. We talked of the *differences between the ways of the spirit and those of the soul.*

Traditionally, we've been taught to distinguish between external realities, things that happen to our bodies, and the inner states of our spirit that are purported to rise above these events in the physical world. Soul is an ambiguous middle ground—neither exclusively material nor entirely abstract—an inner place of imagination that bridges both extremes by "deepening events into experiences."[11] The spirit is usually understood as carrying us up to a place where we see everything in a sacred light.

The spirit transcends our worldly experiences while the soul transforms whatever is human into all that is holy. The soul is the dark and earthy soil where we can cultivate the higher power within us. We get to know our souls by exploring our dreams, fantasies, and imagination—territories where nothing is forbidden.

As Anne gradually accepted the richness of her own soulful ambiguity, she began to turn away from her reclusive, ascetic search for the holy and toward the sweet, natural savoring of worldly delights that included the profane. She became part of a mutually supportive community of artists and writers in which she made both love and friends. Gradually, she learned to accept help graciously and to enjoy being of service to others.

From the beginning of our time together, Anne was fascinated by what seemed to her the contradictory array of objects and artifacts that adorn my office. She often commented on the stones, shells, and driftwood I had collected from the edge of the sea and on the pictures and figures of Buddhas, demons and gods of the Hindu pantheon, Hasidic rabbis, Christian icons, mystical mandalas, dancing shamans, and naked men and women.

Anne decided that this smorgasbord of sacred objects must mean that I was a pagan. Actually, I'd been raised as a Jew, but my parents considered being Jewish an ethnic identity that had more to do with social appearance than with religious devotion.

When I was a child, I told them I wanted to be a rabbi. They made a mockery of my calling and eventually I reacted rebelliously with adolescent overkill by becoming a militantly non-Jewish atheist.

It was not until I met Marjorie, whom I eventually married, that I reopened my soul to religious experience. I was a second-generation Jewish-American from New York whose parents felt embarrassed by my immigrant grandparents' inability to assimilate. Marjorie was a Dutch-Scotch-Irish Presbyterian from West Virginia, raised by a family that prided itself on being descendants of the first white settlers west of the Alleghenies.

When Marjorie wanted to know what it meant to me to be a Jew, I was suspicious. Up until then, the only reason anyone had ever asked me that question was either because they wanted me to conform to some standard of the Jewish subculture, or because they were about to beat me up for being a Christ killer. Marjorie was the first person I'd met who was interested in knowing about my religious commitment simply because she loved me and wanted to get to know me better.

In a way, my patient Anne was right about my being a pagan. Before meeting my wife, I'd sampled atheistic existentialism, flirted with Marxist idealism, immersed myself in the immorality of the French symbolists, and for a while thought of myself as a neo-nihilist.

After meeting Majorie, I explored the more mystical paths of both Judaism and Christianity and gradually became intrigued with mythology, in general, and with Oriental legends, in particular. My exploration of Eastern myths began with southern India's Hinduism. Eventually I met the Buddha—first on the road and then within myself. From there, I followed the route of Buddhism, traveling north, so to speak, through China's clownish Taoism to Japan's zany Zen. Along the way, I studied all sorts of meditation, tried trance-inducing chanting, and abandoned myself to the mad visions of primitive shamans.

Like some other intuitive introverts, I made my own way on an inner journey. One of my role models was Arthur Waley, a translator of Chinese and Japanese literature who did more than any other scholar to take Western readers "madly singing in the mountains"[12] of his imagination. Without ever traveling farther east than Istanbul, Waley managed to accomplish most of his sedentary work in the basement of the British Museum in London.

His approach was completely soulful. Again and again, he would read and reread the original calligraphy of a Chinese or Japanese poem until he felt satisfied that he experienced it as his own. At that point, Waley set aside the scroll and wrote his "translation."

Because of the detachment I have attained from years of meditation, I believe in nothing dogmatically, but I am willing to believe in anything passionately—anything that makes my life more colorful. I no longer make any distinction between the sacred and the profane in human behavior and aspire to a time when "nothing human is alien to me,"[13] because all genuine love is holy. I share Henry Miller's vision of religious experience as seeing " 'GOD IS LOVE!' painted in red on a tenement wall in letters ten feet tall."

My fascination with a soulful side of Judaism that hallows everyday life is a return to the place I started from—

a place at which I arrive again as if for the first time. There is a touching Hasidic tale that illustrates holiness in everyday life—a story about a small village congregation who had gathered together in the House of Prayer on the eve of the High Holy Days. They were waiting for the rabbi to arrive so that the services could begin. Time passed, but he did not come.

One of the women of the congregation began to worry about her little girl whom she'd left alone in the house, so she decided to hurry home to look after her child and to make sure she hadn't wakened.

When she listened at the door of her house, everything was quiet. "Softly she turned the knob and put her head into the room—and there stood the rabbi holding her child in his arms. On his way to the House of Prayer, he had heard the child crying and had played with her and sung to her until she fell asleep.''[14]

PART III

❧

Coming Home,
the Eternal Return

Realization of one's true self is happiness.

—*Chuang-tzu*

The only victory lies in surrender to oneself.

—*Sheldon Kopp*

10

Where Are You in Your World?

A tale is told of a young man called Eisik, son of Yekel, who lived his whole life in Cracow. Years of abject poverty had so sorely tested his self-confidence that he no longer felt he had a place in the community. Things went from bad to worse, but no matter how long the crises continued, they could not shake Eisik's faith in God.

One night, this poor young man dreamed that the Lord told him to travel to Prague and look for a treasure under the bridge leading to the king's palace. Ignoring the ridicule of his neighbors, Eisik set out on the long journey. But when he arrived in Prague, he discovered that the bridge was guarded day and night.

He dared not dig for the treasure, but he was unwilling to leave without it. Day after day, Eisik waited near the bridge, hoping for an opportunity to make his dream come true.

After watching him suspiciously for almost a week, the captain of the guards asked the poor young man whether he was looking for something or waiting for someone to show up. Eisik told the captain about the dream that had instructed him to journey so far from home.

The captain laughed and said, "And so to please the dream, you wore out your shoes to come all this way to Prague. If I had your faith in dreams, I should have had to go to Cracow to dig for treasure buried under the stove in the shack of a pauper called Eisik, son of Yekel."

Eisik listened as the captain mocked his dream, and without commenting, he returned home to Cracow, dug up the treasure from under his stove, and used it to build a house of prayer for his community.[1]

We are better off when we listen carefully to the seemingly irrational guidance that our dreams and fantasies provide. Like Eisik who followed his dream to the place where he got the final clue to the buried treasure, we must be willing to trust what our souls have to tell us. If we are bold enough to explore unusual or even eccentric ways of living, we can "take journeys, confront dragons, and discover the treasure of our true selves.[2] *The dragon we must slay is no more than the monster of everyday expectations about how we ought to live our lives.*

If we are willing to try out our unique and peculiar choices, we'll have to leave behind the comforts of familiar rules and conventions and endure such hardships as isolation and disapproval. We'll also have to find the courage to stand on our own and the wisdom to make our own decisions without any preapproved standards for who we are supposed to be and how we ought to act. *We cannot reach the center of ourselves without seeking the innermost edge of our longings and exploring the outermost edge of our imaginations.*

Once we break the chains of convention, we risk feeling lost, wondering if we're going crazy, and forfeiting the support of those we usually depend on for approval. If we listen to our hearts, we will be sent on soul-making journeys. To pursue to the end these odysseys of transformation, we must make an ethical commitment: *We must know what we feel, say what we mean, and do what we say.* To persevere and progress in search of a self and a life all our own, we must reaffirm this commitment again and again, from moment to moment, for the rest of our lives.

Our self-esteem then is solid, resting reliably on knowing that what we've done is what we truly believe to be right, regardless of the outcome or how other people have judged our actions or what has happened as a result of our efforts. When we reap the reward—discovery of our singular selves—the risks seem worth taking.

Within each one of us there is a pearl of great value. It is solely our own and cannot be found in anyone else. If we are to claim our prized uniqueness, without knowing exactly what we're looking for, we must search our souls for directions, and listen to what our hearts have to tell us about how to find this hidden treasure. This precious pearl that is our individual worth can only be found when we are willing to stand alone.

In times of personal crises we have two fundamental alternatives. We can passively accept whatever happens to us as our fate, or we can actively take on the circumstances as challenges, trying to make what we can of the situations. By consciously choosing to pursue the solitary journeys these crises encourage, *we transform an impersonal fate into our own personal destiny.*

When we reach the end of the unfamiliar paths followed by forging out on our own, we will find that we have come home at last. Yet, our place in the community to which we've returned has been transformed, as well as ourselves. When we reenter the world where we once lived lives defined by other people's standards, we discover a newfound freedom—we're no longer bound by what we once believed was proper or expected. We now know more clearly what we believe in and understand more fully just how we want to live.

But we cannot hope to return home to our own personal place and speak to others in a voice that is truly our own without first leaving their "twittering world"[3] with all its scolding, mocking, and mere chattering. We must be willing to journey alone into that alien land we call our unconscious.

There the parts of ourselves we usually ignore will appear in the form of monsters and ordeals that we will have to face squarely if we are to prevail in the heroic quest to be who we are, no more, no less. We must repudiate our conventional rules of conduct, consider unthinkable thoughts, and ask unspeakable questions—if we are to follow intuitively the ambiguous, unfamiliar guidelines that govern the dark night of our souls. Facing the shadowy demons within us, we come to terms with our fears of being ambushed by them and, as a result, discover an otherwise unattainable, gradually evolving sense of self-assurance. This self-confidence can never be developed completely, but, as a result of what confidence we have attained, we will experience episodes of personal freedom that occur more and more often and last longer and longer.

For example, there are times when we express an original idea to certain people that is out of line with what they take for granted. Their reactions—ranging from raised eyebrows to admonitions such as "How could you even think such a thing!"—impose social pressure on us to retract the idea or to revise our words to be more conforming. But our increased confidence serves to set aside the self-doubts and inhibitions that these pressures are intended to evoke.

Once we have withdrawn to find ourselves and have returned home transformed, we will be back *in* the world, but *no longer of the world*—we will be able to interact with others without submitting to their definitions of who we are supposed to be. Even after we have emerged from the disorder that we needed to experience so we could discover "the still point" at the center of our souls, there will be times when once more we "hear the old voices" calling us away from the core of our true selves. Sometimes, we will choose to go along with the group, but this doesn't mean we've forgotten all we learned.

There is no finish line to cross as we pursue our personal pilgrimage, no state of perfection to attain, no final answer to be found. We are, at the same time, separate from the community and part of it—the traveling and the sense of arrival are inseparable. Still, we find ourselves in a curious position. Although we aren't free of the troubles that life inevitably brings, we realize that they are "experiences common to all." As a result, more often we'll be able to experience crises as storms in the valley viewed from a mountain top,[4] without getting needlessly upset.

Instead of wasting time and energy crying, "Why me?" we will recognize that some problems that have been delivered to us in particular were really addressed *"To whom it may concern."* Even so, we remain responsible for making what we can of anything that may come along.

We remain accountable to the higher power within us
throughout our lives—accountable for who we are and
how we live. A tale is told of a chief of police who came
one night to visit a holy man who had been arrested
because his adversaries had denounced him to the authorities as a heretic.

When the complacent, self-assured, traditionally religious chief of police first entered the cell, the holy man
was too deep in prayer to notice his jailer's coming. Struck
by the power of the prisoner's inner peace, the police
chief began to talk with him about spiritual matters. After
a while, he asked the holy man, "How are we to understand the line in the Scriptures that tells us that the all-
knowing God had to ask Adam, 'Where art thou?'"

The prisoner replied, "In every era, God calls out to
every one of us, 'Where are you in your world?' He asks
His question of each particular person in a particular way.
For example, He might ask you, 'Now that you have lived
forty-six years, how far along have you come?'"

When the chief of police heard his own age mentioned,
the story touched him personally and his heart trembled.
All at once, he realized that he himself was the person
whom God was once again asking, "Where are *you?*"[5]

11

Everybody Wants to Go to Heaven, But Nobody Wants to Die

When I first found out that I was suffering from a life-threatening illness, I felt completely unprepared for the crisis. Confronting seemingly imminent death required more of me than I imagined I was able to do. The acceptance of my fate that I described in the opening chapter reflects a long and hard-won struggle with the painful challenge life had unexpectedly imposed on me.

I'd always known in my head that I would die someday, but thinking of death as *an idea in my mind* turned out to be of absolutely no help. To transform acceptance of dying into an enrichment of living, I had to learn to experience my mortality as *a feeling in my heart*. At the time of the onset of my illness, I was still in my thirties. Certain that my death awaited in the faraway future, all I'd done to prepare for dying was to take out some life insurance.

When I was told that I was not likely to live very long, I felt deeply depressed and desperately helpless. Frantically trying to restore the illusion that I remained in control of my life, I seriously considered committing suicide. When I gave up planning to kill myself, I found ways to continue to imagine that I was more in control of what would happen to me than anyone can ever be.

I decided to donate my body to science so that I could at least attain symbolic immortality, and sent for the required legal forms. For the next two years, I maintained my denial of death by leaving the unsigned agreement out of sight in a drawer of my rolltop desk. When I finally set about to sign the forms, I found myself procrastinating once again.

By then I'd had an elaborate dream about a group of medical students observing my autopsy and seeing me undressed and overweight. The next morning, I decided not to donate my body to science. I was too embarrassed, too vulnerable to allow such an exposure of my frailty, even if it meant that I'd have to give up being immortalized in the history of medical research.

When I sent for the forms, I told my family of my decision. Two years later, I related my embarrassing dream, and declared that I had changed my mind. When I rescinded my plan, and admitted that I had been denying my death, I learned a badly needed lesson about life.

Up to that point, humility was never my strong suit. Earlier, I had instructed my family that when I died, I wanted them to hold an encounter group-style memorial service where everyone who knew me could gather to share their feelings.

It took me a long time to realize that I had no right to

attempt to intrude from beyond the grave. What my family and friends chose to do after I died was none of my business. I let them off the hook, telling them that whatever they decided to do about my death would be all right with me.

As I began to accept the challenge inherent in the crisis of facing my death, I found unforeseen rewards in picking up that gauntlet. I started asking myself just how I wanted to live whatever life I had left. My first reaction came in the form of a romantic image of recklessly riding a motorcycle to the West Coast, where I would begin life anew.

Although I found the fantasy compelling, it struck me as particularly odd. I'd never even ridden a two-wheel bike, much less a motorcycle. To complicate matters further, my illness had impaired my balance so that biking would have been physically impossible. In any case, I never cared much for the California subculture.

As my image of riding off into the sunset receded, I considered some other, more serious alternatives. Did I want to continue my work, maintain my marriage, see the same friends, and spend my time doing what I had done up till then? When I discovered that the answer to so many of those questions was YES!—as if for the first time I recognized how I was happy with much of the life I'd already chosen.

Despite this deeply satisfying discovery, for a while my thinking remained more magical than mystical. For a while, I became uncharacteristically superstitious. At first I was obsessed with matters as silly as how much was left in the large bottle of shampoo I kept on a shelf in the shower. Although I would have denied it at the time, secretly I half-believed that I wouldn't die until the bottle was empty. To ward off the fulfillment of that notion, I washed my hair less often.

Because I expected to die soon, I was reluctant to buy new clothes and so my wardrobe also fell into disrepair. I thought back to my father's death ten years earlier. He'd spent most of his life treating everyone generously—everyone but himself.

He often said things like, "You can only wear one suit at a time," and usually only bought himself things that he desperately needed. I remembered how proud my father seemed to feel when for the first time he bought two suits. He was fifty-eight and he'd indulged himself at last. Two years later he was sixty and he died. I thought, "What the Hell!" and bought myself some new clothes.

I wasn't yet affirming life—I was still deriding and denying death. At this point, my youngest son came to me with a simple, straightforward request that turned out to be a complex gift in disguise.

While my children were growing up, we'd always had cats in the house—as many as five or six at a time. It had been a while since our last cat had gotten lost, strayed, or been stolen. Nick wanted to know whether he could get another kitten. He suggested that if we each got one, we could share the fun of raising them together.

I told him that I wanted a few days to think over his suggestion. Cynically, I thought to myself, "Just what I need! Another creature to love while I live and to lose when I die." Suddenly it struck me—that *was* exactly what I needed! Loving more would help me to feel as alive as I could for as long as I happened to live. Like Molly Bloom in James Joyce's *Ulysses*, my answer became and will continue to be "yes I said yes I will Yes."[1]

I don't remember what Nick decided to call his kitten, but I named mine *Moishe Kepoyer*, which, roughly translated from Yiddish, means "Murray Who Turns Things Upside Down and Inside Out."

Ironically, poor Moishe is long dead and I am still alive. He was so badly torn up by some neighborhood dogs that I couldn't bear to bury him myself. I asked my middle son, David, to dig my kitten's grave while I stood by and cried.

In his innocence, my youngest son, Nick, had been wiser than his aging father. Before we'd gotten our kittens, I had explored in my earlier writings what it meant to me that my death might come too soon. I'd begun to understand that at least I might die well, with grace, and in my own way. When I accepted my youngest son's life-honoring offer, I initiated a stirring in my soul that set off an initially bewildering series of transformation dreams.

My earlier dreams had helped me to prepare myself for dying. At the time these latest dreams began, I was completing a manuscript that was a sort of last rite, a confession of errors.[2] My soul's most recent images turned me toward beginning a new book,[3] one that would further my transformation toward learning how to go on living.

The transformation dreams began at winter's end. Later that spring, I was scheduled for a routine neurological checkup. During this change of seasons, I had been instructed by my doctor to watch for symptoms that might necessitate a third ordeal of brain surgery—the one I was certain would kill me.

The context of all of these dreams was the family's annual trip to Martha's Vineyard Island—our site of summer renewal and the place of my own annual pilgrimage to the sea.[4] In retrospect, I realize that the dreams began at a time when I was anticipating celebrating having lived through yet another medically uncertain year of my life. My birthday coincided with the third anniversary of the last operation I'd undergone.

The dreams were filled with wonderfully powerful images of transformation—great tidal flows, swelling seas, changing landscapes and innovative ways to travel. In each dream, a terrible storm surged and subsided.

When the tempest had passed, the sky brightened and the sea sparkled more beautifully than before the bad weather had begun. At the end of every dream, I became keenly aware that I had survived a mighty blow. Like sea and sky, I, too, emerged in better shape than I'd been in before the disturbance.

Each morning, I had a vivid memory of the previous night's dream, but for a long while I couldn't understand what they meant. I found my bewilderment unsetting but, at the same time, I felt excited.

For several weeks, the dreams recurred as variations on these same themes. Although the particular images changed, the motifs of natural crises and satisfying resolutions remained constant.

I felt as if my mysterious, dreaming self was sending me urgent messages that my reasonable, waking self simply could not comprehend. In desperation, I decided to write to a deeply loving and dearly beloved friend who is a madly poetic, acutely conscious, disturbingly intuitive soul. I had long experienced him as a shadowy guide through the underground labyrinth of my unconscious. He frequently felt lost in the fog he maintained as a buffer between his own inner and outer worlds. At such times, I served a reciprocal role for him.

Before going to bed, I decided that the next morning I would write and request his help in solving my soulful riddle. That night, unexpectedly my own unconscious made the answer available. Before I ever sat down to write the letter, I'd had the final clarifying dream of the series.

The previous day's residue gave shape to that night's illuminating imagery. I had been suffering the final hours of such a bad case of the flu that I'd felt as though I were dying. Off and on that day, I'd found myself obsessing over Eliot's line about the world ending weakly with a whimper, rather than loudly with a bang. Whenever I'd felt well enough that day, I returned to rereading the legend of the search for the Holy Grail.

By evening I'd recovered sufficiently to wash the dishes. On a miniature television set that we keep in the kitchen, I watched an enthralling natural history documentary film about snakes—those skin-shedding symbols of eternal life.

The culminating dream occurred that night. I was getting ready to set out for the Vineyard. As I packed for the trip, I felt a combined sense of excitement and relief—as though I had already delayed that journey too long. At last I was about to get on with it.

In the dream, I was a woman who was having trouble getting her car packed to go. The difficulty centered on my unsuccessful attempts to attach a small television set to the roof of the automobile. I cried out for help.

From far away, but clear enough to be understood, I heard another woman's voice giving me the advice I needed. She told me that if I wanted the television set to stay in place, I had to turn the dial that tuned in the educational channel frequencies as far as it would go.

I wanted to believe her seemingly impractical suggestion and so I began turning the dial as she'd instructed.
When I did, I soon saw many more numbered channels
than I had known existed. The frequencies went up well
past sixty! I was astonished, but went on following her
advice.

When I dialed past channel sixty, all at once the television screen lit up to reveal a bold, clear caption. I understood immediately that this was the solution I had been
seeking—the answer to the riddle posed by my earlier
dreams. The caption read: Without Dying.

I woke up laughing. It was a lovely, bright new morning. I allowed my dawning vision to gradually reshape the
way I'd been leading my life. It was time for me to stop
dying and to begin living again.

With a lot of help from my friends, from my family,
and even from a couple of kittens, my life has been transformed by this crisis of facing my death. Undergoing that
transformation has made me feel more alive to each
moment than I ever felt when I'd half-believed I was
going to live forever.

Hope is not the denial of death. True hope is possible
only after we willingly walk to the edge of despair by
facing all the little deaths in life and the great death that
awaits us thereafter. A favorite line I've repeated before
comes from Martin Buber: It is a glorious thing to be old
when we know how to begin again, not by being young,
but by becoming old in a young way.[5]

The truly joyful person is like someone whose house
has burned down and who begins to build anew out of
the deep need of his or her soul, not as a once and for
all commitment, but as an ever-renewed finding of direction, a response to the call to be heard in each new hour.[6]

All God's Children

Feeling fully alive doesn't depend on what we believe in as much as on the way we live and experience both the great and the small moments of our lives. Crises will continue to occur, and whenever I am able I will meet the challenges that they offer me.

Although I can't literally play the piano, I am determined to let myself be transformed by the sounds arising out of the stillness of my soul and to allow my heart to call the tune to which I dance my life.

All God's children are lost, but only a few can play the piano.

Epilogue

Let this be the end of the book, not of the searching.

—*Thomas Merton*

The spiritual journey is never ending.

—*Sheldon Kopp*

Epilogue:
A Street Guide to the
Higher Power Within Us

1. No matter how well our lives are going, there will be times when we ask ourselves, "Is that all there is?"

2. When you think the meaning of life has been lost, what you need to find is yourself.

3. Everyone feels lost and alone at times.

4. The fulfillment we need lies buried deep inside us.

5. Where are you in your life?

6. Why aren't you more like yourself?

7. If we endure the holy insecurities, we can find the higher power within us.

8. No one else can find your higher power for you.

9. When you follow your heart, you will find your way home to your true self and the people you love.

10. The traveling and the sense of arrival are inseparable.

11. To live your own life, you have to create your own story.

12. If you withdraw from others for a while, you can discover who you are that they aren't.

13. Making an inner journey is a risky business—it can transform your life.

14. The solitary path to the depth of our souls leads us

to the edge of our aloneness and back to a place among others that is truly our own.

15. Every soul has its own shadow side.

16. In the dark night of our souls, we can begin to see the sparks from the higher power within.

17. Trying to will ourselves to be different won't work.

18. The only victory lies in surrender to oneself.

19. All of you is worth something, if you will only own it.

20. Accepting our weaknesses frees our strengths.

21. We all experience predicaments that make us feel upset and unprepared.

22. Every crisis presents a crossroads, and paths open up we may never have seen otherwise.

23. Whether or not life is fair is irrelevant.

24. Asking, "Why me?" is useless. The only question that counts is, "Where do I go from here?"

25. What if God doesn't want us to be caged in our lusts, but to be free in them?

26. Then whatever goes on in our imaginations is nobody else's business.

27. We want so much to seem normal and nice, we're tempted to hide the very things that make us singular.

28. The false images we create to conceal our real selves from others may fool ourselves as well.

29. Until we realize that the monster of others' expectations is just a paper tiger, we remain threatened by their concepts of who we ought to be.

30. When we honor our peculiarities, we can make the most of all the unique things we are.

31. We must know what we feel, say what we mean, and do what we say.

32. Why would God make us all so different and then allow only one way to serve Him?

33. When we act in accord with both our heads and our hearts, everything we do becomes a form of prayer.

34. Whatever we are undertaking at the moment is the most important thing we can do.

35. True hope is possible only after we experience true despair, facing all the little deaths in life and the great death that awaits us thereafter.

36. Feeling fully alive doesn't depend on what we believe in, but on how we experience each great and small moment in our lives.

37. God dwells wherever people let Him in.

38. We can let Him in only where we really stand, where we live a life that is truly our own.

Notes

Prologue

1. Gershom G. Scholem, *Major Trends in Jewish Mysticism* (New York: Scholem Books, 1961), 261.
2. The higher power is beyond gender. For the sake of simplicity, whenever I refer to God, I will use masculine pronouns.
3. Martin Buber, *The Origin and Meaning of Hasidism* (New York: Harper & Row, 1966), 48.
4. Martin Buber, *The Way of Man* (Secaucus, N.J.: Citadel Press, 1960), 40–41. [First published in 1950 by Routledge and Kegan.]

Chapter 1

1. Sheldon Kopp, *Who Am I . . . Really?* (Los Angeles: Jeremy P. Tarcher, 1987), 147–182.
2. Dinner table anecdote, Joseph Campbell with Bill Moyers, *The Power of Myth*, ed. Betty Sue Flowers (New York: Doubleday, 1988), 117.
3. *Ibid.*, 120.
4. Martin Buber, *Tales of the Hasidim: The Later Masters* (New York: Schocken Books, 1948), 173.
5. Martin Buber, *Tales of the Hasidim: The Early Masters* (New York: Schocken Books, 1947), 105.
6. *Ibid.*, 231.

Chapter 2

1. *Ibid.*, 53.
2. Martin Buber, *Tales of the Hasidim: The Later Masters* (New York: Schocken Books, 1948), 177.
3. *Ibid.*, 251.

Chapter 3

1. Derived from Sri Ramakrishna's *The Tales and Parables of Sri Ramakrishna* (Madras, India: Amra Press, 1943), 259–262.
2. Martin Buber, *Hasidism and Modern Man*, ed. and trans. Maurice Friedman (New York: Harper & Row, 1958), 141.
3. Jolande Jacobi, *The Way of Individuation*, trans. R. F. C. Hall (New York: New American Library, 1965), 208.
4. Leslie Fiedler, *Freaks: Myths and Images of the Secret Self* (New York: Simon & Schuster, 1978), 24.
5. Martin Buber, *Tales of the Hasidim: The Early Masters* (New York: Schocken Books, 1947), 315.
6. C. G. Jung quoted in Jolande Jacobi, *Psychological Reflections: An Anthology of the Writings of C. G. Jung* (New York: Harper & Row, 1961), 208.
7. Martin Buber, *Tales of Hasidim: The Later Masters* (New York: Schocken Books, 1948), 306–307.

Chapter 4

1. Martin Buber, *Tales of the Hasidim: The Early Masters* (New York: Schocken Books, 1947), 286.
2. Martin Buber quoted in Maurice Friedman, *A Dialogue with Hasidic Tales: Hallowing the Everyday* (New York: Human Sciences Press, 1988), 76.

Chapter 5

1. Martin Buber, *Tales of the Hasidim: The Later Masters* (New York: Schocken Books, 1948), 248.

2. These pieces were published in *VOICES: The Art and Science of Psychotherapy.*

3. Sheldon Kopp, *Guru: Metaphors from a Psychotherapist* (Palo Alto, CA: Science and Behavior Books, 1970).

4. *Ibid.*, 159–166.

5. Dylan Thomas, "In My Craft or Sullen Art," in *Collected Poems* (New York: New Directions, 1953), 142.

6. Sheldon Kopp, *This Side of Tragedy: Psychotherapy as Theater* (Mountain View, CA: Science and Behavior Books, 1977), 199–200.

7. Meister Eckhart, quoted in F. V. C. Happold, *Mysticism: A Study and an Anthology* (Baltimore, M.D.: Penguin Books, 1967), 72.

8. Martin Buber, *Tales of the Hasidim: The Early Masters* (New York: Schocken Books, 1947), 65.

Introduction to Part II

1. My interpretations owe more to all that Jung's writings have taught me than to what I've learned from Freud.

Chapter 6

1. Martin Buber, *Tales of the Hasidim: The Later Masters* (New York: Schocken Books, 1948), 53.

2. Annie Cohen-Solai, *Sartre: A Life,* Anna Cancogni, trans., Norman Macafee, ed. (New York: Pantheon Books, 1987).

3. Lawrence W. Lynch, *The Marquis de Sade* (Boston: Twayne Publishers, 1984).

4. Annie Cohen-Solai, *Sartre: A Life,* Anna Cancogni, trans., Norman Macafee, ed. (New York: Pantheon Books, 1987), 169.

5. *Ibid.*, 142.

6. *Ibid.*, 76.
7. *Ibid.*, 251.
8. Lawrence W. Lynch, *The Marquis de Sade* (Boston: Twayne Publishers, 1984), 35–36.
9. *Ibid.*, 39.
10. *Ibid.*, 49.
11. The Marquis de Sade, *The 120 Days of Sodom and Other Writings*, compiled and translated by Austin Wainhouse and Richard Seaver (New York: Grove Press, 1966), xi.
12. Simone de Beauvoir, "Must We Burn Sade?" in *Ibid.*, 3–64.
13. The tarot is a Gypsy fortune-telling deck of cards that includes a set of archetypal images believed to be derived either from ancient Egyptian sacred writings or from Jewish Cabalistic magical tracts, and believed to have been brought from India to the West early in the fourteenth century. In any case, they are surely very old, perennially enthralling, and rich in mystic symbols.
14. Ralph Metzner, *Maps of Consciousness* (New York: Collier Books, 1971), 55.
15. Maurice Friedman, *A Dialogue with Hasidic Tales: Hallowing the Everyday* (New York: Human Sciences Press, 1988), 45.

Chapter 7

1. Martin Buber, *Tales of the Hasidim: The Later Masters* (New York: Schocken Books, 1948), 157.
2. Laurie Lisle, *Portrait of an Artist: A Biography of Georgia O'Keeffe* (New York: Simon & Schuster, 1986).
3. Patricia Bosworth, *Diane Arbus: A Biography* (New York: Avon, 1984).
4. Laurie Lisle, *Portrait of an Artist: A Biography of Georgia O'Keeffe* (New York: Simon & Schuster, 1986), 17.
5. *Ibid.*, 137.
6. *Ibid.*, 173 [My italics.]
7. *Ibid.*, 269.
8. *Ibid.*, 276.
9. *Ibid.*, 355.

10. *Ibid.*, 420.
11. Georgia O'Keeffe filmed by Perry Miller Adato (New York: National Education Television, 1975).
12. Patricia Bosworth, *Diane Arbus: A Biography* (New York: Avon, 1984), x.
13. *Ibid.*, 17–18.
14. *Ibid.*, 52.
15. *Ibid.*, 299.
16. *Ibid.*, 155.
17. *Ibid.*, 208.
18. *Ibid.*, 226.
19. *Ibid.*, 265.
20. Robert Motherwell, *The Dada Painters and Poets: An Anthology* (Cambridge, MA: The Belknap Press, 1989), xii.
21. *Ibid.*, xxvii.
22. *Ibid.*, 171.
23. Martin Buber, *Tales of the Hasidim: The Early Masters* (New York: Schocken Books, 1947), 174.

Chapter 8

1. Lanza del Vesto, *Return to the Source*, Jean Sidgwick, trans. (New York: Simon & Schuster, 1974), 225.
2. Peter Goldman, *The Life and Death of Malcolm X* (Urbana, IL: University of Illinois Press, 1979).
3. Abbie Hoffman, *Soon to Be a Major Motion Picture* (New York: Putnam, 1980).
4. Quoted in Peter Goldman, *The Life and Death of Malcolm X* (Urbana, IL: University of Illinois Press, 1979).
5. *Ibid.*, 383.
6. Abbie Hoffman, *Soon to Be a Major Motion Picture* (New York: Putnam, 1980), 58–59.
7. This demonstration against capital punishment centered on the execution of rapist-murderer Caryl Chessman.
8. The hearings on alleged subversive activities in San Francisco.
9. Against the nomination of Hubert Humphrey as candidate for president at the Democratic Convention in Chicago in 1968.

10. Abbie Hoffman, *Soon to Be a Major Motion Picture* (New York: Putnam, 1980), 297.

11. Martin Buber, *Tales of the Hasidim: The Later Masters* (New York: Schocken Books, 1948), 214.

Chapter 9

1. Martin Buber, *Tales of the Hasidim: The Early Masters* (New York: Schocken Books, 1947), 129–130.

2. Thomas Merton, *The Seven Storey Mountain* (New York: Harcourt Brace Jovanovich, 1948).

3. James S. Gordon, *The Golden Guru: The Strange Journey of Bhagwan Shree Rajneesh* (Lexington, MA: The Stephen Greene Press, 1987).

4. Martin Buber, *Hasidism and Modern Man*, Maurice Friedman, ed., trans. (New York: Harper & Row, 1958), 85.

5. The title of Merton's autobiography, *The Seven Storey Mountain*, derives from the seven-circled mountain of Purgatory in Dante's *Inferno*.

6. Thomas Merton, *The Seven Storey Mountain* (New York: Harcourt Brace Jovanovich, 1948), 123.

7. *Ibid.*, 188.

8. *Ibid.*, 423.

9. James S. Gordon, *The Golden Guru: The Strange Journey of Bhagwan Shree Rajneesh* (Lexington, MA: The Stephen Greene Press, 1987), 41.

10. Victoria Lincoln, *Teresa, A Woman: A Biography of Teresa of Avila*, ed. Elias Rivers and Antonio T. de Nicolas (New York: Paragon, 1984), 62.

11. Quoted in *Carl Jung and Soul Psychotherapy*, ed. Karen Gibson, Donald Lathrop, and E. Mark Stern (New York: Haworth Press, 1968), 32.

12. Arthur Waley, *et al.*, *Madly Singing in the Mountains: An Appreciation and Anthology of Arthur Waley*, ed. Ivan Morris (New York: Walker, 1970).

13. Terence, *The Self-Tormentor* in *The Complete Roman Drama: All Extant Comedies of Plautus and Terence, and the Tragedies*

of Seneca, ed. George E. Duckworth (New York: Random House, 1942), Vol. 2, 199.

14. Martin Buber, *Tales of the Hasidim: The Later Masters* (New York: Schocken Books, 1948), 87.

Chapter 10

1. *Ibid.,* 245–6.
2. Carol S. Pearson, *The Hero Within: Six Archetypes We Live By* (San Francisco: Harper & Row, 1986), 1.
3. T. S. Eliot, *Four Quartets* (New York: Harcourt Brace Jovanovich, 1971). The unattributed quotes in this chapter are Eliot's. I owe much of my understanding of Eliot's *Four Quartets* to Elizabeth Drew's commentary in *T. S. Eliot: The Design of His Poetry* (New York: Scribner's, 1949).
4. Carl Jung quoted in Jolande Jacobi's *The Way of Individuation,* trans. R. F. C. Hall (New York: New American Library, 1967), 46.
5. Martin Buber, *Tales of the Hasidim: The Early Masters* (New York: Schocken Books, 1947), 269.

Chapter 11

1. James Joyce, *Ulysses* (New York: The Modern Library, 1934), 678.
2. Sheldon Kopp, *The Naked Therapist: A Collection of Embarrassments* (San Diego: EdITS Publishers, 1976).
3. Sheldon Kopp, *An End to Innocence: Facing Life Without Illusions* (New York: Macmillan, 1978).
4. Sheldon Kopp, *If You Meet the Buddha on the Road, Kill Him! The Pilgrimage of Psychotherapy Patients* (Palo Alto, CA: Science and Behavior Books, 1972), 153–159.
5. Martin Buber quoted and expanded in Maurice Friedman, *A Dialogue with Hasidic Tales: Hallowing the Everyday* (New York: Human Sciences Press, 1988), 150–153.
6. *Ibid.,* 53–54.